HARDSCAPE

INNOVATIVE HARD LANDSCAPING MATERIALS FOR GARDENS

ann-marie powell

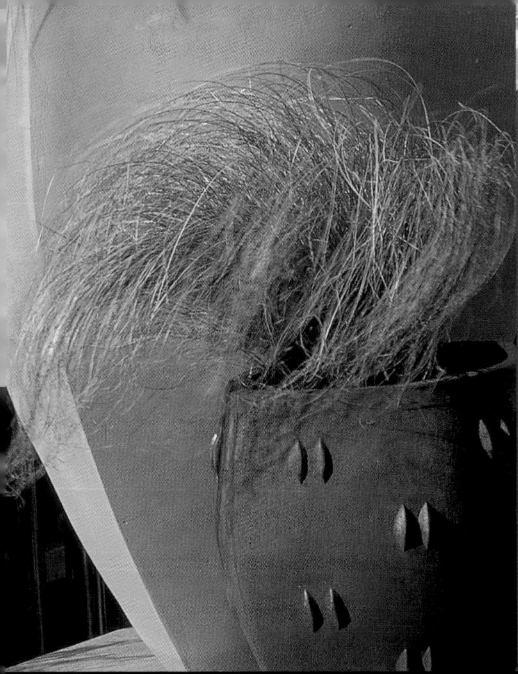

HARDSCAPE

INNOVATIVE HARD LANDSCAPING MATERIALS FOR GARDENS

ann-marie powell

photography

andrea jones

David & Charles

A DAVID & CHARLES BOOK

First published in the UK in 2001

A catalogue record for this book is available from the British Library.

ISBN 0 7153 1008 9

Edited by Clare Hill
Book design by Sue Michniewicz

Distributed in the trade in North America by
North Light Books
an imprint of F&W Publications, Inc.
1507 Dana Avenue
Cincinnati, OH 45207
(800) 289-0963

Printed in China by Leefung-Asco
for David & Charles
Brunel House Newton Abbot Devon

CONTENTS

INTRODUCTION

To me, hardscape, or hard landscaping – by which I mean everything except for the plants and earth – has always been an aspect of gardening I have relished and enjoyed. Hard landscape materials give a sense of permanence, structure and personality that holds a garden together. Hardscaping connects all the elements in a garden by linking the planting and working areas to make a satisfying space in which to enjoy the trials, tribulations and sheer elation that make up a gardener's world.

Uncomplaining and reliable, the hardscape is the engine that keeps all the cogs of the garden ticking over with perfect timing. It creates perspective, rhythm, texture and accent long after the plants in a garden have huddled underground for their winter hibernation. And when the plants are at full tilt, a strong hardscape plays a key supporting role.

We are becoming more and more aware of the blurring of the lines between the garden and house; the architecture of a home is often carried through into the garden, and aspects of the external landscape are often carried inside. Boundaries are being broken down, increasingly resulting in the innovative use of space – and also in the use of fantastic materials, which are springing up in gardens around the world.

I have read many books that celebrate fantastic gardens, both modern and traditional. These are books that glory in the immeasurable beauty of the planting that adorns a space. Their pages are filled with the practicalities of how to lay hard landscape materials, but not one of them satisfies my thirst for materials such as glass, stone or steel, nor my interest in the more unusual approach.

INTRODUCTION

In my work as a garden designer, all too often I have staggered into my clients' homes, quivering under the weight of great piles of suppliers' catalogues, magazines and books that I've littered with page markers. For a long time I have yearned for a reliable and extensive sourcebook to use; a book that allows the beauty of the materials to speak for themselves.

In this book I want to illustrate the growing wave of enthusiasm for materials and their uses, so that everyone can take some element of the hardscape around them and incorporate it into their own personal space. Where possible, I have shown materials used in a real garden situation, illustrating genuine examples and possibilities. I don't advocate that everyone should rush out and rip up their gardens tomorrow – hard landscaping is expensive – but I hope to encourage you to take and develop whatever part of this book, large or small, is appropriate to you.

The book leads from the essentials of formulating plans for hard landscaping use, through practical applications in the garden, and then to a showcase that allows the materials to sing out for themselves. I hope that this arrangement will allow users to dip in and out of the pages as the mood takes them.

But, inevitably, all I can give you are examples – and I am aware that those featured in this book are my own taste – but personality is key to any successful scheme. Everyone is different, and that's the beauty of creating your own garden. It is an expression of you, because you have the final choice about what you do...

Ann-Marie xxx

PART 1

PLANNING & INSPIRATION

It is often the first step that is the hardest when deciding on a hard landscape structure for your garden. Hardscapes are the key to harnessing and holding a garden and its style together, but worries about how best to use the space, how to arrange the required areas of hard landscaping, and how to reach a final decision that you won't regret later are all difficult to overcome. It is often safer to take the easy option.

But, with a little forethought, you could create a space that you relish, instead of one that you simply put up with. All too often decisions about hard landscaping are negatively influenced by limitations of choice, yet affordable ideas, materials and applications are available if you know how and where to look.

To design your ideal space, you need to unlock your thoughts. Working through a process of design before laying that patio or erecting that fence will inspire you to seek out alternatives, ultimately leading to a final decision on design, material, structure and placement that will make your garden work successfully for many years to come.

MOTIVATION

Gardens are many different things to different people: we all get our hands dirty outside for a variety of reasons, and we all have contrasting needs and requirements from the spaces we cultivate. But although our motivations may differ, all gardeners would agree that the link between man and cultivating the ground is intrinsic; man and the earth are unavoidably entwined.

PURPOSEFUL, PLEASURABLE AND PRACTICAL GARDENS

People have always created gardens, but the first gardens were made to satisfy the basic need for survival, rather than the aesthetic or recreational motivations of western gardens today. It is thought that gardens first emerged from the desert, where plant cultivation and crop growth were key to a people's survival in the harsh, arid environment.

Practical gardens that produced food, building materials and shelter began to exist first in Mesopotamia. Settlements began to spring up throughout this region, perhaps as a direct result of the realization that plants could be grown and domesticated to provide a food source.

On the banks of the River Nile it was the ancient Egyptians who were the first to plan and build ornamental gardens. Gardens became associated with spirituality and religion; they were linked with temples, with the plants and flowers regarded as symbols of beauty in their own right. They were also a symbol of wealth. Dating back to 2200BC, gardens incorporated walls for privacy, cooling ornamental pools of water and a variety of surfacing materials. The hard-landscaping features unified these gardens to create spaces that the Egyptians felt were 'a triumph over nature'. These ornamental grounds would certainly have been a lush contrast to the desert that surrounded them.

THE HANGING GARDENS OF BABYLON

Perhaps the first gardens to incorporate vast amounts of engineering and architectural prowess were the fabled Hanging Gardens of Babylon, one of the Seven Wonders of the World. It is said that they were built sometime between 605–562BC by Nebuchadnezzar II for his wife, Amytis. In fact, the gardens did

This garden in the grounds of the Hempel Hotel in London is designed to be cool and contemplative so that those who use it it feel relaxed and tranquil. Although undoubtedly modern, the restful atmosphere is achieved through strong references to Islamic gardens of the past, with their clean lines and reflective pools of water.

decent patio, deck chairs or maybe a hammock, barbecue!

not hang but were reminiscent of modern-day roof gardens, laid out on a series of ziggurat terraces. These terraces were said to be roofed with stone (difficult to source on the Mesopotamian plain) and brick balconies. A huge chain-pump system irrigated the terraces, with bitumen and lead providing a waterproof seal for areas where water was used.

Most of us can only dream of the lavish extravagance that went to make up the Gardens. Today, houses are not usually as large, budgets are definitely limited and we simply don't have the time, space or money to build landscaped gardens on such a huge scale. Our houses spill out into the garden, and every bit of space must be utilized to the full; gardens have become an extension of our homes. 'The outdoor room', is now a phrase that we commonly use to refer to our private garden spaces. Also, our motivations have changed since the ancient gardens of yesterday were built.

However, whatever your own motivations for building a garden, you should not compromise when it comes to your choice of materials, be they plant-based or structural. Plants are easier to change and are less of an investment than the hard structural materials that form the backbone of any garden.

QUESTION YOUR NEEDS

Take a long look at what you want and need from your space. You alone can decide on the essentials, as the domestic garden is a very personal and private plot of land. Whether your garden is brand new or inherited, the keen gardener will want to imprint his or her own touch into the garden

Big Urns, York stone, lovely old brick walls

style as a whole. As a gardener myself, the first thing I consider is what I or my client wants from the space, what needs to be got out of it and how to organize the areas to make the garden successful as a whole.

TAKE A VIEW

View your garden from all angles and at different times during the day, ignoring what is already there, and study it long and hard before you commit to any arduous grafting. Look at the wider landscape through the lens of a camera to pinpoint the highlights of your space. View the garden from upstairs and downstairs, through every window and make sure you assess it thoroughly.

Discuss your garden with visitors – people all have very different ideas and styles and they may recognise an aspect that you have never really noticed before. In your initial consideration and approach to the garden, it is best to rule out nothing and no one. All the input you get will help you decide what you want from your space, and to make your choices about how to carry it out. It can be very difficult to break down a space into working elements when your garden is a blank canvas of green turf, or is crammed with the previous owner's taste, but it can be changed – pathways laid, terraces built and structures erected – to make the garden truly your own. Forget about the plants for now; they are the accessories to a solid, permanent blueprint of hard areas that can make or break a garden's unity.

The wider landscape is an important element in your garden's harmony, but it, of course, cannot be changed. The motivations behind your garden's scheme and your choice of garden building materials can be

above: To entwine both dwelling and garden into the wider landscape, materials were considered from the first in this project in Norfolk. A timber-framed house with linking boardwalk and decks were purposely built to look soft and natural against a backdrop of trees and fields. **right and far right**: In town, urban focal points, hard, straight lines, and materials in the wider landscape can be utilized to create a garden that sits well within its surroundings.

influenced strongly by whether you live in the town or the country. A rural situation may encourage you to create a more natural, undulating scheme that nestles tranquilly into the landscape. At the opposite end of the scale, however, a deliberate interruption to the landscape can be startling and beautiful. For example, a brightly coloured concrete installation that breaks up a drystone wall in the heart of the countryside demonstrates a stark awareness of rural space and, to me, illustrates the relationship between man and nature. It may also question our sensibilities: how and why did it arrive?

Town gardens have very different vistas from rural spaces, and highlighting aspects in an industrial landscape can create a contemporary mood. For me, the highlight in a friend's garden is the steel-stepped fire escape of the apartments opposite, and I long to accentuate this view through the use of similar materials in her space.

Underwater garden with psychedelic fish, bubbles and stuff

PEOPLE: THE KEY TO ANY GARDEN

Take ten people at random, give them one of ten identical houses, with ten identical plots of bare earth attached, and a budget of precisely the same amount of money, and ask those ten people to build a garden that they think is best suited to that environment.

I guarantee that if you went back a year later to examine the progress made, you'd be shocked and surprised. Every garden would look completely different, they would be in different stages of completion and each would have a very different emphasis. This is because at the crux of the modern-day garden phenomenon is personality. Gardeners have always, and will always, use the garden in the way that works best for them. And we're all different.

However, no matter how carefree or lackadaisical the personality, in the construction of a garden space there will always have to be some organization or planning. Consciously or subconsciously, some kind of hard landscaping – be it garden division, screening, boundary or surface – will have been considered. This may be down to utilitarian reasons (privacy, plant protection, and so on) rather than the aesthetic, but it is simply common sense to consider materials and their arrangement at some stage of the game. However, if hardscaping is more strongly deliberated from the beginning, rather than as an afterthought borne out of necessity, the garden will be an infinitely more aesthetically pleasing, user-friendly place.

Swinging garden chair with ice cream van

FORM AND FUNCTION

An area of hardstanding surface is usually one of the first considerations. That's because, no matter how eager a gardener you think you are, life in the garden without a hard surface can be miserable. A terrace, pathway, patio or yard is a useful area to work on, makes access far easier and can be the best place to relax and enjoy the view.

Hard surfaces make life easier. Walking on grass or bare earth can soon produce a muddy quagmire. But hard surfaces, or for that matter any kind of hard landscaping feature, does not need to be purely functional: they can provide visual interest through texture, colour, and winter presence, becoming indispensable in a garden's overall look as well as being practical.

Intimate brick terrace and teak furniture for dinner parties

MAKING CHOICES

However you decide to use your outdoor space, the choices made will have to be approved by all the people who use the garden; the garden must be practical, desirable and hardworking for everyone. This means giving some serious thought to your lifestyle and the way you in which you, your family, roommates or, indeed, animals, intend to use the garden on a day-to-day basis.

Because of the common problem of confines of space (particularly acute in towns and cities), privacy, solitude and adaptability are all important considerations, but the wish list could go on and on.

Something funky – maybe some neon lighting and a light-up outside dance floor!

Cost For most of us, budget is an important factor. The cost of materials is something that very often decides our final choice. But that doesn't mean that we want the materials we use to look cheap. One of the aims of this book is to show not only aspirational ideas, but also imaginative uses of everyday, accessible products that can give a garden a truly creative edge.

Durability When we have committed to our choices we, quite reasonably, will want them to last for a reasonable amount of time. Although we are beginning to realize that a garden does not come for free, we will have yet to embrace the idea that a garden can involve a large financial commitment. However, once we have made that commitment, whether it's a large or small investment, we want it to last.

Maintenance With our busy lifestyles, many of us want to have the time to sit back and enjoy the garden, instead of perpetually working on it. Relaxation time is precious in this all too frantic world, and we want to be sure that, whatever materials we decide to use in our outdoor rooms, we will have the time to really enjoy them, and perhaps to entertain in them with family and friends.

A mellow garden with lots of wood and railway sleepers. I'd like a treehouse!

Self-expression I always think writing a list of motivational reasons – things that really drive you to want a garden, and reasons that you want to use your garden for – is extremely important. Your list could include wanting somewhere safe for your children to play; using a material that will show off your plants to their best advantage; a desire to express yourself through your garden design; wanting somewhere to grow your vegetables; or simply a place where you can enjoy being outside. It might be important that your garden includes aspects of religious, spiritual or historical importance, too.

Practicality Practical considerations are really down to common sense. Choices involve selecting the right material for the job. Would gravel really be appropriate outside the back door where your children run in and out all day? Would it be best to use a pre-formed pond liner? Can you get the materials into your space without too many problems? Access can easily be overlooked. If you can only bring materials through the house, should you really be ordering those huge slabs of York stone?

Goldfish, dry ice, glass block walls, and shimmering water

Aesthetics In the past, only materials found or produced locally were an option, so picking and choosing wasn't such a problem; you just had to use what was available. Today, mass transportation and new technologies have increased our options, so we have the luxury of making our choices based largely on aesthetic considerations.

WHY, WHERE AND HOW

Think carefully. The ingredients of surfacing, boundary, structure and other hard landscape applications really set the tone in a garden. They are the bones that the rest of the garden hangs from. Hard landscape materials give the garden a distinct style, and the choices you make are ones you will have to live with.

Materials are expensive, but if chosen wisely, and installed correctly, they will last for many years, providing countless hours of immeasurable pleasure. Finding out the why, where and how you want your garden will help you to plump for a hard landscaping option that works best for you; you just have to put some energy into finding out what it is that really flicks your switch.

Grecian urns, pillars and statues, maybe a roman mosaic

STIMULATION

The creation of a garden is a process that has many layers. It is important to work through all these layers in order to reach a satisfactory final decision on the look of your space.

above: Found materials can provide attractive focal points. The ingenious placing of this piece of sand and sea-worn brick walling is extremely effective. **left**: An alternative use of washers, when used *en masse*, creates an eye-catching, humorous surfacing material that literally tinkles underfoot.

This process is a technique that professional garden designers go through almost automatically during the development of any space. So, having deliberated over your space and how it works (or will work) best in the first chapter, we now move to the next layer: finding inspiration for your choice of materials.

Inspiration can be discovered almost anywhere while you are considering your hardscaping choices. I think it is a mistake only to look at readily available garden resources. Other people's gardens, gardening magazines, television programmes, the local garden centre and gardening books are obvious places to turn when we are moulding ideas for how we would like our garden to look, and yes, they are fantastic reservoirs of inspiration, but I'm adamant that when marvellous and inspirational 'ready-made' designs are placed in front of you like a cake on a plate, it is all too easy to reach forward and grab a piece of them! The brain is quick to process the image of agreeable gardens (either consciously or unconsciously), and elements of these gardens are suddenly translated to your own, before you have explored other, perhaps more fitting, alternatives. I would like to encourage you to try to take your thoughts elsewhere when you first think about your own space. Don't turn your back on the more obscure.

COLLECT YOUR THOUGHTS

Start by looking into yourself; sit down with pen and paper and rummage through your backpack of personal experience to find what you have subconsciously filed in the part of your brain marked 'garden'. You may come up with a wealth of possibilities straightaway. If not, then begin to log what you see when you're out and about. Recording your ideas is extremely useful. I for one, find it almost impossible to carry visual images in my head. I carry a notebook, and quite often a camera, so I can scribble things down or capture on film places I've visited which I know I'll want to be reminded of in the future.

The more ideas you collect, the greater the resource you can dip into later, so you can really develop the garden of your dreams. While I am not advocating that you should think about gardens and gardens alone (after all, it is my job to do this!), I encourage you to collect scraps of information, magazine cuttings

above left: Look out for inspiration when abroad; this holiday snapshot might not astound friends and relatives, but it may certainly be useful when redesigning your garden landscaping! **above right:** A pad brimming with your own notes, together with reference books and magazines, are indispensable when exploring hard landscaping materials and applications. **below right:** Historic applications of hard landscaping materials were once also considered revolutionary. This stacked vertical slate flooring, now covered with the moss of ages, was once crisp, new and fresh. Slate is infinitely adaptable and would be appropriate today.

and samples that have brought you to this point of building a garden of your own. Collecting your thoughts (be they positive or negative) about your garden will become a scrapbook of concepts encompassing all that you might want. It's almost like looking at a collage of your ideal space, which will ultimately develop into a garden you will really want to embrace.

When I visit my clients they sometimes seem uneasy about their own ideas, thinking that they sound silly, that their ideas aren't developed enough to share, or that they would be impossible to create because of physical impracticalities or budgetary constraints. But I find this the most stimulating part of the design process; anything is possible with a little forward thinking and planning. For this reason, you should try to give the ideas that stimulate you as wide a range as possible. Refuse to limit yourself when you think about what you would like to influence your garden. At this stage of the design process you should rule out nothing and have confidence in what you like. There are several starting points.

LOOK BACK TO GO FORWARD

Looking to the past for inspiration is not a modern idea; Edwin Lutyens (1869–1944) often looked back into history and echoed architecture from days long gone. He revelled in the use of hard landscape materials and used them sympathetically and successfully. Lutyens and the garden designer, Gertrude Jekyll (1843–1932), together embarked on a great partnership, and fine examples of their work can be seen at gardens such as Munstead Wood and Hestercombe. The use of stacked vertical slate as a surface is a technique that Lutyens often used, and it has persisted through changing fashions in garden design. This type of

above: Materials used in unusual ways can make powerful visual statements, as these upright chunks of stone (circa 1902) illustrate. **left:** This now disused summerhouse would have looked stunning when first built. Thought to have been designed by Edward Lutyens, the slate surfacing is stamped with his trademark of stacked slithers of stone.

surfacing is not only attractive but also provides an excellent non-slip finish that can be easily integrated into a garden of today.

Traditional materials and their applications could also be turned on their head to create new and innovative effects. Keep a good look out for pieces of architectural detailing that catch your eye, be they in gardens or other examples of building. Taking photographs or making sketches will ensure they aren't forgotten, so that if you are not going to build the garden yourself, they will be very useful to show to your landscaper during your garden planning discussions.

But, although the past does hold much to appreciate, many would like to see gardens moving forwards. They would like to see modern, contemporary spaces truly reflecting the world we live in now. Ironically, this is not a new or revolutionary idea. In the 1930s, an outspoken young garden designer, Christopher Tannard, felt gardens were 'not of our time but of the sentimental past'. He felt that if people found pleasure in machines, abstract paintings and tonal experiments, as well as natural objects, then these should influence the garden, too. Looking to the past need not lead to reproduction as, on a different level, it can help immensely. I agree with Tannard completely.

THE EVERYDAY ENVIRONMENT

Gardens are becoming an arena where a wealth of different disciplines mix together: traditional crafts meet modern metalwork; sculpture sits comfortably alongside the flowerbed; and show gardens are filled with unconventional influences. It seems natural to look further afield when considering real spaces at home to such things as buildings and structures (be it at home or abroad), interiors, workshops and yards, and art in the myriad of materials that artists use. Considering such abstract things as texture, shape and colour are most important too; just a glimpse of a deep-red Indian fabric has inspired gardens before now.

However, using too many ideas and, therefore, materials in one place can result in an area becoming confused and distorted. A balance does need to be found. As much as I relish contemporary design, I do not want gardens to be solely championing hard landscape materials as king, even though we should not underestimate their importance. We cannot ignore the fact that hard materials are the very bones of a garden. They often initiate a garden theme, they are indispensable in creating scale and proportion and, in essence, an atmosphere that grounds a garden to its environment and surroundings. At last, hard materials are being given more thought, and it is important to consider them as beautiful in their own right.

Pylons Municipal features in today's landscape can be surprisingly influential in a garden that finds the balance between hard and soft landscaping. The relationship between man and the environment has been a consideration of many landscape architects and designers since gardens first began. This battle can

be seen across the country: pylons stamp their way through fields and towns alike, yet I cannot help but find such a relationship interesting. Inspiration can sometimes come from the most unlikeliest of places. To me, the taut cabling of a pylon gives an impression of strength and support. The steel used in a pylon's construction could create a glistening structure echoing the frost in winter when, in a garden environment, there is not much to look at other than hard materials.

But it's not just the cables that I find inspirational in high-tech constructions; most technological apparatus and space-age buildings are both sculptural and fun. Often the architects have combined materials so successfully that it would be a crying shame not to echo this new modernism in gardens, too. In towns, this approach to the urbanization of gardens can be extremely effective.

From high tech to traditional, it's not just futurism that turns me on. Many different styles and features within buildings can inspire. Timber has been used structurally in buildings around the world for centuries, and the same is echoed in the garden. Historically, wood has been easy to get hold of and is reasonably priced. Yet in spite of this, many basic garden structures have not changed in decades. Trellising is a good example. Styles have remained the same for what seems like forever, and although we have become attuned to painting or colouring our trellis in some way, most people stick to pre-fabricated designs and pre-stained colours because it's easy.

Wooden rafters I have found pure inspiration from looking at the rafters of a disused barn. With its generously dimensioned beams and rafters showing wood in the raw, its timbers with their open weave, and the shafts of light that pierce the spaces where the roof tiles have fallen away, the barn led me to believe that more imaginative trellising can be achieved. Spinning the age-old timber construction of trellis on its head can create a much more interesting weave.

Bespoke trellis is becoming more and more accessible as competition by suppliers increases, and trelliswork is so easy to assemble yourself. However, there is no reason why designs shouldn't be a little more inspired. Use batons with unusual dimensions spaced to create a very open or tight weave. Use a backboard to close off some of the openness, but allow spaces here and there so plants can hang on and light can pass through.

Why stick to the ubiquitous square or diamond designs? A trellis of pure verticals or horizontals can look fantastic. Use bent or reclaimed wood to take away the ordered, symmetrical

opposite: Although abhorrent to most, when looked at closely it can't be denied that the engineering used in this power station can be hugely inspirational to modern garden design. **above:** Construction design throws up many ideas that can be used in smaller scale garden building. The rafters of this neglected old barn show the strength and durability of timber that could be harnessed in the structure of a pergola or trellis. **left:** A walk around a builder's yard can be wildly stimulating. Materials abound and combinations can be tried out on site.

effect, or a mixture of timbers to create a tapestry of latticework.

BUILDERS' AND RECLAMATION YARDS

While looking for other materials in builders' merchants and yards, keep your eyes peeled for other sources of inspiration. Materials are stacked up as far as the eye can see, and contrasting and complementary materials can be sought out and compared. Staff will also advise on the appropriateness of materials for your chosen application.

You can often pick up samples of materials for very little and then take them home and experiment with them. Live with them for a while and see how you feel about them before committing yourself to building, laying your surface or whatever else you're planning. With a little bit of searching and some creativity, you may find materials that you never knew existed.

The materials you are tempted by need not be new. Many different materials can be packed full of character, and if you can spare the time, a good place to begin to look for quirky one-offs is in scrap and reclamation yards. The materials' tones and different hues of colour seem more intense when looking at those that have stood the test of time. They exude a feeling of longevity that more space-age materials lack.

Rust As materials get older, they can be utilized to magnificent effect. Objects lying waste can be manipulated to make them look visually stunning. Rust, for example, although an organic process rather than a material, has a very definite place in the use of hard landscaping materials today. Rust can enhance a garden's originality, creating unique effects wherever it is invited in.

Practicalities should also be considered when looking at using recycled materials. Obviously, using corroded metals to create a seating area could be wholly inappropriate, but as an ornamental material to use in planters, obelisks and other decorative effects, the rich oranges and reds, alive due to the oxygenating process behind a metal's decay, can create a fieriness that is still soft and warm and contrasts beautifully with planting. Recycled materials can be an easy way to achieve an individual space with the minimum of cost.

left: The delicate filigree and colourful tones of rust has provided stimulation to many land artists, sculptors and garden designers – and it's easy to see why. **below:** In one of my gardens a smattering of colour is provided by plastic furniture and flooring to add vibrancy to an urban space.

INSIDE-OUT

The phrase 'the outdoor room' has become one that we are very familiar with now, and though the phrase has perhaps become over-used, I feel that this ideal is one that is brimming with common sense. But we shouldn't just look at materials for the garden that have always been meant for external use. After all,

to inspire us. For example, if you have a particularly pleasing archway in your house, why not carry these proportions outside in the form of a pergola or other structure? A terracotta or stone floor inside can blend with similar outdoor 'flooring'. Key colours can be transported to the garden in the form of hammocks, throws, pots and furniture.

Furniture can be truly transitional. Many products that are second nature to the interior can easily be adapted to, or simply used for, outdoor living. Why not consider using a wooden chest of drawers in the garden? It could look stunning, with the drawers used as vessels to contain plants. When looking at an object we have used for years, it is difficult to imagine the same thing for any other use.

Over-familiarity can become a problem; even materials suppliers are not always open to unusual applications. We tend to be scared of change and a bit nervous of new ideas or

above: Echoing architectural details from inside to outside links the house and garden together. Shown perfectly here, the detail of the window is reflected in the pergola outside. **right:** In his inspired mosaics, Kaffe Fassett certainly takes the inside/outside link to the maximum with the inclusion of the handle from an old cup!

the garden is decorated in much the same way as an interior room, and many functions are echoed inside and outside: an indoor carpet acts as a floor covering in much the same way as an outdoor surface does, and walls provide a boundary and privacy both inside and out.

Patios and terraces have long been used as outdoor dining rooms, so why not expand this link between inside and outside further? Many building materials that are not traditionally used in gardens could be used more to create a truly contemporary feel. Rubber, plastic, metal and glass can all be used outside to fantastic effect, and there is a plethora of innovative indoor architecture interpretations. If you keep an open mind at trade fairs, interiors outlets, or when looking through brochures, catalogues and magazines, you'll be surprised at just what can be used.

ART

Gardens are becoming more and more widely accepted as an art form. In fact, I believe that gardening is a form of art, and there is no reason why we should not be influenced by art in our treatment of hardscape designs.

Art has always influenced designers in whatever field they work. The ways artists use materials to realize their work is, I believe, very similar to the way in which garden materials should be used. Artists often just look at the material and have ideas about the way it can be moulded to give the effect they are looking for. They brutally discard superfluous doubts and concentrate on the useful and positive.

Gardeners have long been attracted to art for inspiration, as have artists long been attracted to gardens. The English artist and film director, Derek Jarman, was spurred by a simple piece of flint discovered on a beach. He brought it back to Prospect Cottage, his seaside home in Dungeness, Kent, and after adding a single piece of driftwood and some stones with holes in them, his garden had begun. A simple beginning, using found objects in the garden to harness a creative impulse, has resulted in the creation of a domestic garden space that is probably now one of the most famous in the world.

PERSONAL SANCTUARY

A garden should be a place of personal sanctuary. It should be somewhere that you can go to feel relaxed, stimulated or contemplative. Whatever you want from your garden, try to keep an open mind to all the many different influences that exist around you.

When you really believe that you've considered and understood your own feelings and needs about your garden hardscape, as well as having exhausted all avenues of inspiration while making up your mind, you will then have to progress to the next step and start thinking about how you are going to realize your aspirations.

Using ordinary fencing wire, this delightful urn, created by the artist James Price, is extraordinarily beautiful.

INVESTIGATION

By now you should know your garden, with all its strengths and weaknesses, inside out.

Your inspirations have been formulated, expanded and then pinned down to the few that really excite you.

Now is the time to begin nailing down some kind of plan as to how your garden will look. No matter how dull and time-consuming it might seem, it is most certainly worth the effort required to draw up a plan of your garden space. Once drawn up, your plan will become an indispensable tool for finding out exactly what you are working with, and where best to place pathways, seating areas, screens and so on. You will be able to use the plan to work out the quantities of the materials you would like to use to build your garden. This in turn will enable you to make an accurate estimate and to ascertain if your ideas are truly realistic with regard to your budget.

above: A finished design or plan of your garden, marked with all the intended features and landscaping, is key when thinking through spatial use and practicalities. It will also become immensely useful when estimating and ordering quantities of materials. **right:** Available from builders' merchants, 30m/100ft tapes are by far the easiest to use when measuring up a garden.

MAKING UP A PLAN

You may already have a garden plan that was drawn up when making other alterations to your property, or you may have an outline plan included in your property deeds. If not, to take the

headache out of measuring and drawing up a plan yourself, there are surveyors who will accurately measure a garden for you. This service will allow you to feel completely confident that all dimensions are accurate. Remember, measurements are crucial and can stop or lead to mistakes, but if you feel confident enough, grab your tape measure and get measuring!

Draw up the measurements taken using a ruler and pencil on a piece of plain or graph paper. You will need to use some type of scale; perhaps the easiest is 1cm to 1m (1:100)/1in to 1yd (1:36). Try to be as accurate as possible to give a true representation on paper of your garden's dimensions, stopping to check and re-check measurements as you draw them up.

Include as much peripheral information on your plan as you feel is necessary. Indicate where the good and bad views are in the garden, soil type (pH, sandy, badly drained, for example), aspect, sunny or shady spots, boundary lines, existing structures or planting that you want to leave, any slopes, and all the services, such as gas and electricity cables that are so easy to forget. All these things are important to design the garden as a whole, but they will also be a vital consideration when choosing your landscaping material. Don't add anything to the plan that you are not going to keep – why bother? Additions of this kind will simply confuse you when creating something new from your garden.

Consult suppliers for advice on materials. Many are happy to advise you on how appropriate they are for a particular job.

Remember also to ensure that all your landscaping comes within planning regulations and laws. It is a good idea to check if any large and old-looking trees have preservation orders on them. If they do, there is no way that you'll be able to cut them down to make way for your rose arch, no matter how fabulous that rose arch would look!

Once drawn up, or received from your surveyors, it will appear that there is a lot of blank space on your plan, but it may now be obvious how you want to compose your new space. The plan will show the dynamics of the environment and indicate how to use your garden to the best of its potential. It may be a good idea to put pen to paper at this point while you are still fired with enthusiasm. As soon as you do this you'll probably get a gut reaction about whether the garden draft feels right for you. At this point you can make all your mistakes and not worry about costly errors. With the adrenaline still pumping, it's a good idea to begin the detective work that will take your ideas into reality before you make any final decisions.

MATERIAL RESEARCH

When researching materials, advantages and disadvantages of a chosen item start to become more obvious. You will begin to be in contact with experienced tradesmen and women who are used to dealing with the material that takes your fancy on a day-to-day basis. You would be crazy not to take advantage of their knowledge. At this stage, ask them about the qualities that the materials possess, the advantages of a certain finish, gauge or size. Perhaps they will offer you alternatives you had not considered before, and almost certainly they will give or send you brochures or, better still, a sample, to think about. They may even suggest ways to install your materials, and advise whether that installation is best suited to the professional rather than the amateur.

A good place to begin when doing your research is your local garden centre or DIY store, which today can offer a

The key to finding the right materials for you and your space is through research. Visit your library or borrow books from friends to keep costs down.

constantly improving range of materials. If they do not stock the one you want they should be able to give advice on suppliers, or even order it in for you.

There is a host of different research options. Look through garden magazines that you especially like. Often, materials shown in features have lists of suppliers and their telephone numbers. Books often have suppliers' details, as do television programmes and the books or booklets that accompany them.

Ordering suppliers' brochures, then having a good old hunt through them, is a good bet for locating what you want. They will show you colour ranges in the product and the sizes available, and may even unveil some new ideas to you.

New websites are being created all the time, and these are a fantastic resource, allowing you to see what you are looking for almost immediately. A list of some of the websites available today is given at the end of this book.

Look in your local phone book and get on the phone. If you can afford it, there are hosts of craftsman out there who will make to order whatever you want: trellis, metalwork, furniture, garden ornamentation; the list is endless. Speaking to these dedicated and meticulous tradesmen can lead to an idea you have being expanded and developed as the creative partnership forms between you, the originator of the idea, and them, the facilitators. Craftsman love flexing their creative muscles and will probably become as excited as you about the effects you are aiming to create.

DIY OR PROFESSIONAL DESIGNER?

If you have the time, the imagination and the patience, being your own designer can be an exhilarating process. But we are not all so self-assured or handy enough to execute our ideas ourselves. If you just don't feel confident with your drawing or design skills, bringing in a professional garden designer is an option. They are trained to interpret your ideas and turn them into a reality. Ask around for a recommendation or do a little searching to find out their contact details if you see schemes they have designed in the media. They could well be more approachable and more reasonably priced than you imagined.

If your budget doesn't stretch to the luxury of a designer, ask around for recommendations of a good landscape company that specializes in the design of gardens. A builder may guarantee that he will do a good job of making your ideas a reality, but he might not be especially sensitive to your own garden's requirements.

After all the research, the next thing to do is to turn your ideas into reality.

Ok, so I know this is a picture of me, but if you find designing your garden a logistical nightmare, it might be worthwhile employing a designer to do it for you.

COMPOSITION

By this point you'll have probably collected a mass of supporting material, advice, estimates and prices from suppliers. Now is the time to bring all of these things together to decide how your garden will ultimately look.

The best way to start is to eliminate some of your possibilities. Lay out on a table only everything that you can't bear to live without. There may still be a vast array of ideas, but you'll need to slim them down. It's decision time! To help organize yourself, bear in mind when thinking about hard landscaping materials that there are really only two indispensable elements: surface and boundary. All the other elements – structure, ornament, light and water – are merely extensions of these and should be considered in more depth when the outline is nailed down.

If you're not employing a designer or landscaper to interpret your ideas, you now need to start drawing up a more accurate plan for yourself. Grab your garden survey plan (after all, it is a true model of your existing space in miniature, without all the features you no longer want), and take several photocopies of it so you can experiment with the possibilities of your space. Now you can really start to get to grips with the landscaping features that you need and those that you would like to incorporate.

above: A designer will provide you with a professionally laid out plan. If you're doing it yourself, a rough outline plan would suffice. **left:** It may be that you want to re-landscape a whole area, or only an area within it. Either way, it is worth measuring the whole site in order to get the proportions of your new landscaping just right.

The first thing to think about is the seating areas. You might want to sit in the sunny south-facing area of the garden, or to be tucked away under the bower of a tree. Often it is the site itself that determines what is and isn't possible in your choice of hard landscaping. For example, it may be impractical to build any kind of solid structure in a really boggy, wet area; or stone or loose gravel may require the installation of drainage below ground to capture excess groundwater in a damp area, an expense that you may decide is too excessive to consider. In this case, decking may be the ideal alternative. When constructed upon upright 'legs' sunk into the ground and held in concrete, decking has almost no contact with the ground below and is the perfect material for bypassing tricky areas such as uneven ground or wet areas. Indeed, because of their 'floating' nature, decks are ideal for reaching into the heart of the boggy planting space that you have planned for the future.

At the other end of the spectrum, existing level areas of concrete or hardcore used to construct patios, terraces, or walkways can be utilized as foundations for new surfacing materials, often allowing them to be laid directly on top. If this is a possibility for you, ensure that the new patio would still be at least 150mm (6in) beneath the damp-proof course of the house walls to avoid any problems with damp arising from your thrifty moneysaving.

Once you have marked where you want to sit on your plan, you can start to link these areas with pathways. This will give you a more solid idea of what your garden will look like, and what you like the look of. You'll start to see patterns emerging and you'll begin the process of bringing together your ideas.

CHARACTER

The character you want for your garden determines many of the choices you will later make. You may have already decided whether you want a very formal or extremely informal space.

Formal gardens Gardens of this genre tend to be very symmetrical; straight lines bisect each other to create partitions, axes and focal points. Clean and orderly, gardens of this style are a good use of a small space, where the garden can be viewed as a whole. A formal style will pull the whole garden together, making everything in the space so much more obvious to the onlooker, and the hard landscaping choice as a frame for planting becomes key. Anything too busy will detract from the cool tranquillity of the space. Stone, brick or gravel will work best, as they have done for centuries. But, such gardens are not always the low-maintenance option they appear to be. They will work best if kept clean, so keeping gravel or other paving free from leaves or debris can become an on-going battle.

left and below: These two gardens from Chelsea Flower Show 2000 UK illustrate perfectly the difference between formal and informal styles, although both use similar elements. The first has crisp, clean outlines but the second has looser, sweeping curves to give a much more relaxed atmosphere.

Informal gardens If, like me, you are simply too untidy to manage a stable, manicured space, a more laid-back approach may be for you. Informal gardens are just that; they include great sweeps of curves, a much more unpolished approach and are generally more forgiving. The site itself governs the framework of hard landscaping, so the taming of areas is governed by the elements in, or directly affecting, the garden itself. A path may swing round a pool, through a marshy area and into the hot, dry area of the garden where the path itself expands into a patio.

Mixing styles Of course, it is often the case that we choose to have a combination of the formal and informal; a formal area of hard landscaping anchoring the house into the garden can be a good transitional area to settle the building into its more informal outdoor counterpart. Close to the house, it's a good idea to choose the same materials as those used to build the house itself, thus creating a skirt of fluid movement down through the walls of the building and into the earth. Further away, the landscaping can soften and develop more of its own character, and materials can change as often as the atmosphere of the overall scheme does.

Once you have experimented with various different connotations, not forgetting the more humdrum aspects of life such as the washing line, binstore, compost bins and shed, make sure your ideal garden is drawn up exactly to scale, so you can then be ready to mark it out.

MARKING OUT

Marking out is the process whereby you transfer your overall plan onto the actual ground. Once etched on the space itself, it's a perfect time to deliberate over the exact dimensions.

There are lots of techniques used to mark out a garden, ranging from pegs and string lines to laying out using hose-pipes. But, to be honest, I find the easiest way to see a good, clear representation of the garden floor-plan is to outline using a product called spray or speed line, available from most DIY and sporting stores. They are coloured chalk aerosols that allow you to spray out every detail in your garden quickly and with incredible visibility. Don't be alarmed: it is not

above: String is often used for marking out a design on the ground. Once laid out, walk the site to see if your marked out dimensions feel right. **below:** Make sure you are completely organised before starting any hard work!

permanent, so it will not affect any landscaping feature that you wish to keep. You'll need to drag in a friend to hold one end of your tape measure and the stringlines that you will need as a stencil for your spraying frenzy, but, if you've used the scale of 1cm/0.4in on your plan to 1m/36in on the ground (1:100/1:36), this is not an arduous task. The secret is to be patient and keep checking and then re-checking your measurements.

TRY IT OUT

Once you have finished, admire your handiwork from the ground and also from the upstairs windows. Walk the paths, put out a table and chairs in the garden to see if your seating area is large enough, and make sure that these areas are all in proportion to each other.

You'll often find that you want to make changes to the plan once you've experienced how the garden will look when it is built (you have to use quite a lot of imagination for this one!), but this is the best time to make final adjustments. Don't forget, it's more difficult to change your mind once you've started work on laying the foundations.

COMMITMENT

When you're happy with the visible layout, you need to make a final commitment to your choice of materials. Once you've made your decisions, order up the materials and start preparing yourself to get stuck in to all the hard work!

When ordering up materials, most suppliers are more than happy to estimate the quantities you'll need if you supply them with the correct layout dimensions. If you are lucky, they may even work them out for you from the plan that you have drawn up. Remember: they want to sell you their stock, so often your supplier will be happy to advise, source and estimate quantities for any supporting products you may have forgotten about such as mortar, foundations and fixings.

If you're employing a team of landscapers, you can just sit back and watch them do all the hard work for you!

BUILDING

Now you're ready for the building. I want to repeat, however, that you should only build a garden yourself if you are entirely confident of your abilities to carry out all the hard work. When working with hardscapes the labouring is unforgivingly hard, and any mistakes can be potentially very expensive and, at worst, downright dangerous.

If your scheme is particularly complex or above your level of DIY expertise, this is the time to hand over to a contractor so that they can get cracking. Pick one that has been recommended to you or which is affiliated to a landscaping association. Get several quotes, but don't necessarily go for the cheapest, as estimates with extra costs may also point out the extra quality of the work. If you have opted for a contractor, all you have to do is sit back and watch your garden emerge from the earth.

PART 2

PRACTICALITIES

When thinking about a garden in hard landscaping terms, it is often a good idea to break down all the structural components into their separate areas. Pinpointing different hard landscaping applications and uses of materials will put every bit of space under the microscope. When all these areas are considered on their individual merits, one can consider how they will co-exist and work together.

If you are replacing just one element of the garden, for example a fence or a patio, I hope that this section of the book will help, inspire and inform you to rejuvenate an existing garden just as much as it will aid in the creation of a new garden from scratch. All too often when replacing just one garden element, it is tempting to replace like with like, but I hope I can help you break this habit and begin to reinvent a space that will be more considered, more desirable and more personal to you, the gardener.

SURFACE

Surfacing incorporates a massive range of applications such as paths, driveways, steps, terraces, patios and work areas. They each have very different demands and expectations, and, although appearance is very important, it is the texture of a material that will govern your choice.

It may be easier to illustrate this by giving examples. A children's play area needs to be as non-slip as possible, but it should also be soft enough to cushion a fall. On the other hand, a formal seating area needs to be level to accommodate furniture, be easy to clean and should link the garden to the house. So, while wood play-bark chippings would be perfect for a children's garden, they would be texturally challenging for a formal seating area, where stone paving slabs may be more appropriate.

Some surfacing materials are designed to discourage people from walking over them. Stacked stones, expanses of raked gravel and loose boulders take on a sculptural quality, proving that surfaces can be visually stimulating and not just practical.

The main areas within a garden that generally need to be given a hard surface can be broken down into three categories, each with their own demands in terms of suitability of material.

- Areas for relaxation.
- Utility areas to house dustbins, to pot plants and to work generally.
- Access areas that will link all these other areas together, usually recognized as pathways.

These can be broken down further into three considerations that influence the choice of surfacing material: practicality, aesthetics (both also include textural considerations) and finally, cost.

PRACTICALITY

A surface needs to work hard and it needs to do its job well. And, although a good, practical surface needs to be hardwearing, a lot of the trust you put into a material of this nature relies on the construction and application of the material itself. It is certainly worth investing effort into the preliminary groundwork to ensure solid foundations or using a contractor with a good reputation. Remember that the cheapest quote you get for hard-landscaping work is not necessarily the best, and could result in extra cost to you later due to shoddy workmanship.

The selection of a material is influenced by the use of an area. Driveways have extremely heavy loads to bear, and therefore require much stronger foundations than a patio or path. More flexible materials such as gravel or interlocking clay pavers are often used because they spread a car's weight over the driveway surface but both these materials, like all driveway materials, will still need deep, strong foundation materials.

When planning a path or patio, texture is more important for these more frequently used spaces. Textured materials are needed for sloped, ramped or slippery areas to provide a non-slip finish and they can also slow down or speed up 'traffic' over a surface. An evenly laid area of concrete will allow the user to move quickly over it, but a cobbled surface will be more difficult to walk over and therefore will slow traffic down. Colour and pattern, as well as being decorative, can also have a practical application: light-coloured paving will brighten up a shady corner, while a pattern will give a surface a sense of activity that can be good or bad, depending on how the surface is used.

Think also about how your choice of hard landscaping materials will affect your surrounding environment. Even though your garden may be small, ground that is covered with non-porous paving laid on a cross-fall to keep it free from water will still affect the way that your land works in terms of water run off. This may affect the amount of water on flowerbeds surrounding your terrace or the amount of water creeping into your neighbour's garden. If you live in a very wet area, it may be wise to consider slate shales, gravels or the inclusion of a drain at the edge of any landscaped surface.

AESTHETICS

As with most hard landscape choices, the style of the house and its surrounding environment is the obvious starting point when you are considering your options. For example, if you used modern, coloured concrete slabs in front of a period home they would look horrific. As a general rule of thumb, local stone is more sympathetic than imported stone when in a rural setting.

With the vast range of surfacing materials available to us now through the greater ease of transportation, a garden can easily become a hotchpotch of ideas and materials. If a garden is large, there may be a temptation to include as many different materials as possible. While innovation is to be encouraged, having some restraint on the number of materials used in any one space should also be exercised; well chosen, simple materials with a maximum of two, or at most three, surfacing choices in any one area will work best. Consider also the unit size of the paving material you are going to use and keep it in proportion to the size of your garden. Use brick, terracotta tiles or granite setts in a small space and it will appear bigger, but great expanses of York stone could overpower.

Driveways are most successful when only one material is used, with some kind of edging at its perimeter to hold it all together. This restraint makes the area recede. Fussy designs for utilitarian areas make them look too much of a feature. You want to lure visitors into your house, rather than have them be overwhelmed by an ambitious ornamental parking area!

Back in the garden, many people feel that surfacing materials should not impinge on the garden but should be a quiet, supporting accompaniment. However, in more ornamental areas I feel that although a surface should not take centre stage, there is no reason why it cannot have more status in the overall style of a garden, setting the tone for the rest of the space if this is appropriate.

above: Contrary to popular belief, surfacing materials don't have to be dull. A mosaic of brightly coloured tiles adds a burst of brightness.
left: Claire Whitehouse's Chelsea, England garden shows that surfacing can be used as a flat plain. Here she experiments with the texture and tones of contrasting and complementary hard landscaping materials.
right: For the more industrious gardener, bricks clad with copper sheeting are an inexpensive way to introduce metal flooring.

THE RECLAIM GARDEN

Recycled materials carry baggage; worn in and comfortable, they instantly make a space appear warm and inviting. There is real pleasure in taking something that's been thrown away and re-using it for a new and different purpose. With imagination and persistence (reclaim materials can be stubborn when trying to coax them into a new role), highly individual looks can be created from thrifty buying.

far left top: Decking overlaps the pool in a staggered random finish. In various guises, timber encircles the area; even the water feature is constructed using an old wooden board. **far left bottom:** Industrial cogs are given a new vitality by mixing them with recycled glass chippings. **left:** Old railway sleepers (ties), stacked one on top of the other and braced with fixings, become an inviting new bench. **below:** Warped pieces can become focal points in the garden. **right:** Hard landscaping and plants compete for space, creating a terrace that appears to hide in the undergrowth.

Start rummaging through reclaim and salvage yards and you might get much more than you ever bargained for...

Timber is perhaps the most available and obvious recyclable material; notched and worn, previous lives are stained into its grain. Leaving wood as untouched and raw as possible gives a solid, original look. This garden uses salvaged timber to tremendous effect. Floorboards are laid at angles and fixed in a seemingly random fashion; boards appearing to crash and collide into each other. This would look appalling if built using new wood, yet here it simply adds to the charm. If a piece of wood is warped or it's dimensions are uneven, this makes the garden seem more quirky and individual; pieces like this are worth looking out for.

Designs using reclaim materials always work best if they are informal. Eccentric, old materials don't like to conform to the strict confines of formalism! Delighting in the warmth and tones of aged timber, this garden was no more than a year old when photographed but it looks as if it had been there forever.

The planting complements the materials perfectly, further softening the edges of the scheme. I think the recycled timber needs this loose, plentiful planting style; one is the backdrop to the other. Here, the hard landscaping creates an environment that, like an old armchair, is comfortable and snug to sit in. Combined with a water feature, the effect is simply sublime.

This playground surfacing combines several different types of safety surfacing, including wet-pour rubber, playtiles and artificial grass.

COST

That all-important factor, money, has to be considered at some point. Surfacing materials can be extremely expensive because of the area they span and the amount of unseen materials and equipment required, such as foundations and tools. Yet all too often garden owners make the mistake of building their terraces too small. You should remember that your patio needs to house chairs, tables – and people – comfortably, and even though you may save money in the short-term by constructing a small seating area, in the long-term you'll wish you hadn't. Always ensure that there is enough space for people to move around easily.

A certain regard must be taken for the age-old adage that in the end, you get what you pay for. Garden flooring, as with all other hard landscaping in the garden, can be seen as an investment. It adds more living space to a home and value to a property. If selected and then installed with care, a well-considered choice could last for decades – so invest wisely.

Nevertheless, a beautiful surface does not need to cost a fortune. If you simply cannot afford a large financial outlay, an investment of time can reward you with an innovative and creative surface that you might not have achieved if you had just thrown money at your space.

SLABS, SETTS AND TILES

Stone slabs or flags Stone is desirable because of the way it effortlessly rests into a landscape. It is very attractive and has a superb natural finish that gives a timeless appearance, but we have to pay for this privilege. Because they are natural, stone slabs are perhaps the most expensive form of paving. It may be wise to investigate sources of reclaimed stone, as it can be slightly cheaper

Surfaces don't have to be constructed using only one material; combining different materials can often lead to stunning results. **above:** Here, everyday concrete is integrated with grass to give a modern twist. **right:** Glass set amid concrete pavers highlights the curve of the step-over water rill.

than new stone and using it is also environmentally friendly. After all, stone sources are not renewable and this is a form of recycling.

Paving slabs are available in innumerable colours, sizes and shapes, ranging from local stones such as Purbeck and Portland in Britain, through York stone and slate to gravel bond. Quarried stone may be split and then given a sawn, planed, rubbed or riven finish. Always check with your supplier whether the stone you choose is liable to become slippery when wet; if it is durable; and whether it is liable to fracture in frost.

When used for paving, generously proportioned stone flags look far preferable when laid simply in bold, large areas. Some people like the look of crazy paving, but designers advise you to keep it away from the house, because 'it is very informal'. However, I would not recommend the use of crazy paving at all unless you are entirely confident that this is the look you want to achieve; after all, how do you imagine it got its name?

Pre-cast concrete slabs Today there is a massive range of pre-cast concrete slabs spanning the colour spectrum that are more affordable than stone. They range from cheap, soft-moulded versions to more expensive dense, hydraulically pressed slabs. Concrete slabs have had a bad press but they are the most commonly used surface material, and it is easy to see why. There is a wide range of sizes, colours, shapes and finishes available. Finishes range from brick and cobble to more random textures emulating natural stone. Textured slabs provide a non-slip finish, and are produced by grinding the surface off their equivalent, smooth-topped versions, or by pressing in a texture when in the mould. A riven finish made in this way helps to recreate a more convincing imitation of natural stone at half the price. Other finishes include brushed and polished, or exposed aggregate (for that retro Seventies look!). Good quality slabs should be of an even thickness and size, which makes levelling and laying them much easier than slabs of natural stone.

If possible, try to view wet slabs before making a choice as, once wet, they may appear totally different and sometimes completely inappropriate. Also, view a broken slab, as the inside can give a good indication of strength: soft slabs often have a good proportion of large aggregate stones bound in an open-textured, weak mix and are therefore more likely to crack.

Good-quality slabs are extremely dense, comprising an even mix of fine crushed stone and cement with well-machined edges. A broken slab will also show the quality of dyes used in the manufacturing process. A slab that has been coloured all the way through is far preferable to a slab with a surface dye that may chip or fade away.

Natural-coloured slabs are far preferable to garish shades of yellow or pink as these latter can become visually dangerous, clashing with furniture, plants and practically everything else in your garden.

Concrete This is fast becoming an extremely desirable paving material. It can be manipulated and moulded into more fluid shapes, yet is solid once set. It can be dyed with specialist colouring pigments, then polished, brushed, or sawn to produce attractive textural effects. The use of expansion joints (which enable large expanses of concrete to expand and contract without cracking) can produce architectural lines through the surface. Practically anything can be pressed into the surface: sticks, stones or glass can all be used. Whilst travelling in New Zealand, I saw the inventive use of concrete impressions everywhere; leaves, feathers and flowers had been firmed into the surface while the concrete was still damp and then brushed away to produce attractive, permanent collages.

Glass blocks, when used as a surfacing material, can look very dramatic. They are usually cast into reinforced concrete at the factory to provide extra strength.

Glass blocks Glass is becoming more and more desirable as a flooring material. Formed into blocks, it can be used as a surfacing material, but be sure to check with manufacturers on its suitability, as some types of block are only made for walling. To ease construction and ensure safety, glass block surfaces are made into panels with concrete surrounds by the supplier in the workshop. They are then dropped into position later.

SMALL UNIT PAVING

While large paving slabs incur the expense and problems of cutting to fit into areas, small paving units can be combined to interlock in different ways, quickly creating patterns in surfaces to change the look of a space. Dramatic effects can be achieved. Basket-weave or herringbone give static, highly patterned surfaces which hold the eye within an area, while strong, linear patterns will energize a path, creating movement and a desire to move over the space.

Clay or concrete pavers When selecting a manufactured paver, think about texture, colour and style and plump for the paver that best reflects the style of the house, the mood of the garden, or a combination of both. Pavers have a variety of surface finishes including stable and tile imprints to expand the range of brick replicas. Brick or clay pavers are fired to make them harder than walling bricks. They are also are thinner and longer. Because of the speed and ease of laying (less excavation is necessary for foundations) the more expensive can be offset against labour costs, which, once tallied up, can make paviours cheaper than brick. An alternative if you need extra strength is to use engineering bricks, which are very durable.

Brick Using a similar walling brick to the house is a sure way of integrating building and garden. Facing bricks can give an exact match to the walls of a house, although they are often not recommended for exterior flooring as they sometimes flake or crack with frost. However, this effect can look great if it is an antiquated 'been down for ever' look that you want. Bricks can be laid face down, showing the bedding face or on edge.

Granite setts Consider long and hard before using granite setts as they have a strong, urban feel, and the stone is not native to lots of areas. They can be cold and grey when used *en masse*, but look fantastic as edgings to other surfacing such as gravel. Granite, however, is a very expensive material.

Terracotta and tiles As a surface material, terracotta and tiles are becoming more and more popular, and for many they are the ultimate flooring tile between house and garden. Giving a warm, homely feel reminiscent of Mediterranean courtyards, they can add impact to small spaces. Many terracotta tiles are not frostproof, so this should be checked before buying. A variety of non-slip finishes are available; some are glazed or have reliefs stamped into them, giving a more individual appearance.

MODULAR PIECES

Gravel, bark chippings and, more unusually, glass chippings, can be used to fantastic effect to create loose washes underfoot that are perfect for an informal setting, creating a fluid flow around the garden. Larger pebbles can be used to create cobbled paths, and mosaics can be created with various materials such as pebbles and broken tiles.

above: Engraving terracotta tiles makes them more individual and distinctive. Simply take them to a local stone mason. **right and below:** The array of finishes available gives terracotta hugely different looks. But, patterned tiling over large areas can be too attention-seeking, and is so best kept to edging or as detail within a larger area.

Gravel Less formal than paving but crisper than grass, gravel gives a relaxed feel to a garden. It is cheap and easy to lay, and provides a texture that is as much at home in an urban setting as it is around a country cottage. It comes in different sizes, the larger 20 mm (¾in) size being more useful for driveways. It is a perfect complement to planting, providing ideal conditions for seed germination, and it also acts as a mulch for mature plants.

When laid loose, gravel is perfect for awkwardly shaped areas, or in areas where few plants will grow, such as under trees. Available in a large colour range depending on the parent stone, gravel is usually available in three different forms: self-binding,

left: Binding gravel and pebbles together keeps loose materials in place so that intricate patterns can be created. Contrasting shades work well here to create a strong feeling of movement and fluidity. **above:** Chipped stone is more angular than gravel, making it more stable to use for a walk area surface.

stone chippings and pea shingle or very fine gravel. Pea shingle comes from gravel pits and riverbeds and its smoothness is acquired through water action. Because of its round shape, it moves quite easily and so should be retained with an edging strip. Stone chippings or shales are taken from the quarry and then crushed. Many different colours are available, depending on the quarry the chippings have come from. However, be aware that light colours can produce glare in very sunny spots.

Self-binding gravel (for example, Breedin or hoggin) is a naturally occurring material that is spread loose in layers and then compacted using a vibrating plate (which can be rented) to form a solid, but permeable surface.

False streambeds made of gravel can be used to suggest the flow of water and are generally used more sculpturally than as a practical walking surface. Who would want to walk over a well-constructed bed of this kind where each stone has been selected individually or when the surface has been meticulously raked to create rippling effects?

Mosaics Set into concrete, larger pebbles can be used to form mosaics, providing excellent non-slip finishes. Pebbles are available in such a wide range of colours that they can add a burst of life into paved areas, providing relief in the form of decorative mosaic, adding direction to pathways, or emphasizing a visual axis towards focal points.

Broken, coloured tiles can be used to make mosaics that will take your breath away. Also, if you put colour in your tile grouting by adding a brightly coloured paint (blue or yellow, for example), it will effortlessly pull together a wealth of different colours and designs.

Bark chips Used in the same way as loose gravel, bark chips are a fluid material that is fantastic in play and woodland areas. Available in many different grades to suit different purposes, a specialist play bark is perfect for children's areas. Bark chips are becoming more widely available dyed in a range of vibrant colours – but they are not for the faint hearted!

Glass chippings Crushed, recycled glass can be used in the same way as gravel to provide a whimsical, watery effect where water cannot be used, or a glistening, jewel-like surface that shines in the sunlight. Used in shady areas, glass chippings can create a sparkling glow that appears other-worldly, as in Andy Cao's Los Angeles garden, where massive quantities of crushed clumps of opaque glass create a surfacing effect that is astonishing.

Glass chippings are recycled by a process of crushing and then tumbling at high temperatures to create small fragments without sharp edges. It can then be laid loose or bound together to create a fresh new surfacing ingredient for the garden.

TIMBER

Timber, although a hard surfacing material, gives a soft, earthy feel to the garden. The most prevalent use of wood in garden flooring is as decking, but don't lose sight of other options, including the use of natural logs and bark chippings (see page 40). Timber looks fantastic next to water and stunning next to swimming pools.

Timber decking There has been a sharp rise in the use of decks everywhere, as we have increasingly realized the strength and versatility of such a surface. A deck can be extremely successful in creating a level area outside a

below: A chequerboard effect of crushed glass interspersed with the plant Mind-your-own-Business *(Soleirolia soleirolii)* creates a striking flooring, reminiscent of a cubist painting. **right:** Reclaim floorboards give a contemporary look to the deck. Shattering the edge, rather than cutting it straight, emphasises the pool and water feature beyond.

house if the garden slopes dramatically away from the house. Decks and boardwalks provide fantastic covering for rough terrain and can be used to traverse bog gardens or extend into water. For a split-level house, a deck that extends the upper living area can be useful, and because timber is lighter than brick or stone, decking is particularly useful for urban roof gardens.

A brilliant way to get changes in garden levels without having to excavate large amounts of earth in the process, is to introduce decks at different levels. However, when laying your deck, you should bear in mind that if your boundary line is the standard 1.8 metres (6ft) high, a deck laid too high will shift your seating area upwards, raising you up sufficiently enough so that the street or your neighbour's garden is in view – and vice versa.

Decking is also great for areas where a more solid surface such as a York stone terrace would need to incorporate retaining walls, foundations or a soakaway, which is not necessary for decking. These advantages mean that although timber can be expensive, there are less labour costs involved in construction. Also, due to their ease of laying, the amateur DIY enthusiast can build them quickly and easily.

Timber decks can be constructed from hardwood or softwood, giving a variety of colour and graining, but always check that the wood comes from a sustainable source. Timber planks that have been rough sawn, rebated or sandblasted provide non-slip surfaces, stopping the wood from becoming too slippery.

Always lay decks at a slight camber so that water can run off the surface, and ensure there is an air gap between each board to allow for drainage, air circulation and expansion and contraction of the wood. On low decks, it's a good idea to spread a sheet of weed membrane covered with fine gravel under the decking before building as this will help to prevent weed growth in an area that would be difficult to maintain. If the deck is quite high, think about what to do with the ground beneath, as this area is often forgotten and just becomes 'dead' ground.

left: Decking can be laid at almost any angle and cut to create any shape imaginable. Fixings such as nails or screws should be equally spaced to ensure a professional finish to the deck as a whole. **right:** Wooden setts are relatively new to the marketplace but are a tempting alternative to the plethora of decking that has recently appeared.

Decks can be laid down into almost any shape imaginable; you don't have to stick to the ubiquitous square or rectangle. Cut holes through your deck to plant through, or build your deck around the base of a tree to make strong architectural features of plants. For a less uniform look, try varying the widths of the timber planks by using recycled, treated floorboards, recycled scaffold planks or thick, chunky railway sleepers (ties).

Fixings, such as screws and bolts, can add a whole new dimension to decking when they are used loud and proud, as they can contribute to the design by creating patterns that are practical as well as beautiful. Applying paints and stains will inject colour into decks, while still allowing the grain of the wood to shine through.

Decking tiles These give a similar effect to decking planks and can be used to create a chequerboard effect. The tiles are supposed to make laying much easier by reducing the amount of cutting required. However, because they are smaller, they need more support with extra battening underneath them, so they can end up being just as much work.

Sleepers (Ties) Strong, masculine decks can be created with railway sleepers, which are also useful for uplifting and punctuating large areas of gravel or brick as they tone in well

Railway sleepers can be immensely useful when used as a directional inset for a path. When laid across the path they slow the pace down; when laid in the direction of movement, they speed the walker up.

with the ochres, reds and yellows of these materials. They can also add directional movement to paths, affecting the speed with which you walk over the surface. If they are laid across the direction of the path, they slow the user down. However, if they are turned to point in the direction of movement they will speed the user up. (Planks of timber or full-rounded rustic poles can be used to the same effect.)

Log slices Running through lawns or woodland areas, log slices can effectively suggest a path without becoming too heavy. The logs are sawn end-on, so that the natural grain of the wood is able to sing through.

Timber setts Cubes of hardwood cut to produce timber setts are very durable. They echo the more traditional use of granite setts but provide softer, though still very hardwearing, surfaces.

PLASTIC AND METAL SHEETING

These non-traditional materials are well worth investigating. They will give you some great results and provide a really contemporary look.

Plastics Synthetic materials, such as Astroturf®, can inject humour into a garden space. They are available in a variety of colours, textures and sizes of 'grass blade'. Plastic sheeting with raised circles to improve grip can be used as a temporary surfacing. A client of mine used some to cover a shed roof! I am about to cover all the paving slabs in my rented space to create an unusual, brightly coloured external flooring that I can easily lift when I move.

Metals We are familiar with the use of embossed and textured tread sheets, often used in spiral steel staircases, but they are not used much in garden surfacing. You would think that these surfaces become very hot in strong sunlight, but in my experience this is not the case. The main consideration with

Metal grids suitable for flooring are usually made to measure, making them hugely expensive. Look out for alternative grids in DIY stores, as materials not designed for use in garden landscaping are often appropriate to it.

shiny surfaces of this type is glare. However, used sparingly, in much the same way as plastic sheeting, sheet steel can look stunning. In Le Jardin de l'Atlantique in Paris, the use of steel mesh underfoot was an imaginative way to use an alternative material in great curving, sweeping pathways.

EDGING

The perimeters of any hard landscaping material usually need some kind of edging to keep the surfacing in and the rest of the garden out (although, sometimes, this is not always the case). An edging material can complement, contrast or be quietly hidden from view, depending on the desired effect, and almost any material can be used, from a soldier course of brick, through to a curving timber edge or a strip of steel at the edge of a border. They can be used to provide mowing strips for areas of grass, or made to fan out from an area of hard landscaping into the borders, creating a flow of materials in the overall hard landscaping plan.

Attention to detail through the use of edging can add polish and finish to a space, and give a visual flow to hard landscaping. However, if well supported by a mortar 'haunch', some materials can forego the use of edging and spread into other areas of the garden without restriction.

STEPS AND RAMPS

Links between different levels in a space should be given as much consideration as the rest of the surfacing in your garden, as they are a continuation of it. Standing at the top of a flight of stairs, the garden spreads below you; at the bottom, you cannot see what lies ahead until you make the ascent, and this adds a degree of tension, drama and excitement.

Steps can be used as a stage for plants, interspersed with low-growing plants in between the cracks in the paving, or as casual seats. They can also be important focal points, drawing the eye to become unavoidable features. Try to keep outdoor steps as wide, low and gentle as possible so that they will be both easy on the eye and on the feet! Steep steps will encourage fast movement, but in the garden as slow a pace as possible is generally preferable.

Any material designed for surfacing can be used for steps, but use materials that blend in with the other hard landscaping features and with the style of your space. Where space is limited, you can tuck the steps into a corner or, if you're a bit more adventurous, cantilever the treads from a wall.

Ramps can add drama to a garden, drawing the eye into a space. However, they also have a much more practical advantage in allowing access to areas of the garden that are difficult to reach. This is particularly so for disabled gardeners.

BOUNDARIES

Physical barriers in the form of a fence or wall are vital to any garden. In towns they keep the world out and, in some cases, keep the garden in. In the countryside, however, you might want a boundary that allows the natural views into your piece of cultivated ground. Consider the job your fence needs to do: is it to screen, provide security, support plants or filter wind?

Gone are the days when a low picket fence would be enough to mark your garden boundaries. Today we need to feel secure, safe and private in our postage-stamp spaces. But why do we feel the need to board ourselves into our already small spaces with mass produced fence panels?

Garden centres are crammed with ready-made panels, and they're quick and easy to put up; you can replace your fence in a weekend without too much effort. But fencing is not especially cheap, and costs even more if you get contractors to erect it. Now I, for one, don't want to make the kind of financial investment that results in nothing more than a dull, brown expanse of a barrier without eliminating all other options first.

I'm not advocating that everyone goes out and rips out their perfectly adequate fence next weekend, but if it needs replacing, why not use something a bit more interesting than the

ubiquitous larchlap? There is a wealth of products on the market which the consumer is just not aware of – and transformation of an existing fence is easier than you think. If replacement is simply not an option, customize what you have; there are lots of ways to steer your garden away from the packing-crate confines that most fences seem to create.

The space within the home is generally used to its maximum potential, just as gardeners generally give careful consideration to the space in their plot of land, both for planting schemes and structural elements. What really hits me, however, is that the boundary itself is often ignored, put up with, and left to its own devices. As the largest vertical expanse within a garden, comparable to the walls in a house, I am baffled why fences are not used to better effect.

Not all of us are lucky enough to have a high brick wall around our garden's perimeter, but this is no reason to be unimaginative. Smothering a fence with climbers is a good idea, but plants take time to grow and, until very mature, their flowers will pull the eye towards the very fence line that you are trying to conceal. Paint or woodstain will make a fence more appealing until the climbers get going, but there may be another more interesting material to use for fencing that does not necessarily need plants as a foil.

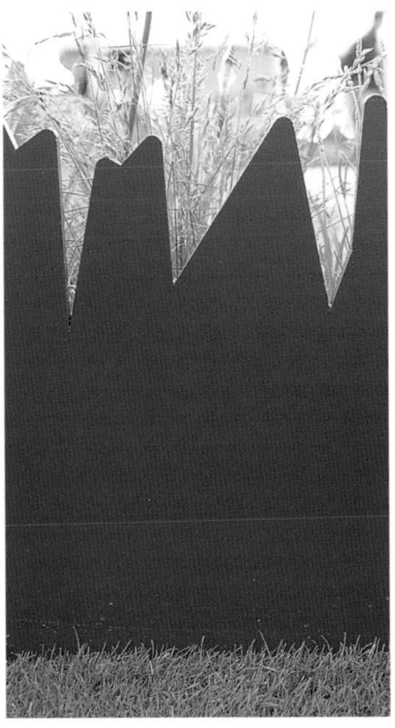

above: Picket fencing as an informal garden divide can be enlivened by a coat of wood stain or paint. Choose tones that complement existing or planned planting. **left:** If your budget allows, large upright slabs of polished stone look spectacular as solid boundary walling, providing a sense of permanence and strength. **right:** This bespoke Perspex fencing makes a modern boundary material that can be cut to any shape and manufactured in any colour you desire.

FENCING

Where privacy or security is important in order to keep the world out and the garden in, solid panel fencing is essential. Whether it is the dreaded larchlap panel or otherwise, a fence can be easily supported on a series of upright posts with customized hangers or simply screws and nails. But more decorative panels of stripped willow, hazel or bamboo use this construction technique too, so there really is no excuse not to get a little creative with your boundaries.

Manufactured panels of bamboo, willow and reed arrive in rolls, which are then stapled or tied over the basic post and arris rail structure. But, if you're revamping an existing fence, panels can simply be covered over, changing the garden mood in a mere matter of hours.

Screening and open-weave Bamboo screen panelling is available in different widths of cane which are split or unsplit. Bamboo is the perfect foil for strong architectural planting, adding

its own texture for the plant to contrast against, and certainly it adds a strong Japanese feel. But, somehow, I prefer willow. It is more contemporary in look and is not so readily 'themed' as bamboo. Willow, with its hues of rusty brown, orange and plummy-red, settles almost anywhere and is equally at home in town as it is in the country.

left, above and right: Natural materials such as hazel and willow were traditionally woven into hurdles to provide a warm and inviting garden backdrop. The popularity of such materials has resulted in willow, stripped reed and heather being available as ready-made screens. Simply roll them out and staple to fencing supports.

Bales of unlinked bamboo, willow or hazel canes can be used to create a similar but looser, more informal feel compared to manufactured sheets of the same materials. If using bamboo, it is essential to cut the canes (or 'culms') just above a joint to prevent moisture collecting in the hollow stems. After that, the sky's your limit – tie it into any design that takes your fancy, using wire or heavy twine to lash the stems together to create an unusual trellis effect. This technique can be applied to almost any material that is available in thin lengths, such as battening, doweling, copper pipe or strong rope. Visit a timber yard or DIY store for inspiration.

Semi-transparent, more open fences such as these can be erected if your garden is used by children as well as adults, as you can see what the children are doing while still giving them some privacy. This type of fencing is also ideal for screening compost heaps and sheds, or if you feel like temporarily cordoning an area off for a particular use. Buy pre-woven hazel panels (or hurdles) to filter wind and therefore protect young plants and vegetables. They are also perfect for climbers to scramble up and, because they are easily moved, they can quickly conceal any horrors in your garden that you don't want anyone else to see!

Much has been made of the longevity of such natural panels but, in truth, this is highly dependent on the particular area and use. One way to extend their life-span is to ensure that panels are not quite touching the soil level; if they touch, rot will quickly set in as it does in any timber. For a 'living' fence, hammer lengths of bat willow *(salix caevula)* into the ground. They will sprout to make a green, leafy screen.

Post fences Fences can be created by just using the posts, without any panelling or screens, in areas where privacy is not of great importance. This open construction of uprights is perfect for internal division too, where a suggestion of division,

left: In this garden designed by Cleve West, upright railway sleepers (ties) have been concreted into the ground to make a loose boundary that is dynamic and bold. **below:** Varying the tops and widths of each pale provides rhythm and movement to a picket fence.

rather than enclosure is required. To do this, sink the posts in at varying distances or intervals, or if you have the luxury of space, avoid a straight line along the boundary divide and instead create a random, rippling effect. The boundary in Cleve West's garden at Barnes Wetland Trust in London is a great example of the open fence. He uses slanting railway sleepers (ties) at the garden's edges, which soar skywards to give the feeling that the garden does not end but moves up into the air.

Posts can be linked together with wires to give privacy yet still retain an open feel. In a town garden, experiment with thick-gauge wire bound tightly between thick 10 x 10cm (4 x 4in) posts to give an architectural, urban feel as the posts draw the eye skyward. Wire could be substituted by rope to give a nautical theme that looks great with expanses of wooden deck. Full timber rounds can be butted closely together to create a rustic, textural, post-only fence.

Fence pales: varying the shape If this relaxed attitude toward security is just not practical, use individual pales (lengths of uprights) nailed to your basic support of post and arris rail to provide a contemporary spin on the traditional picket fence. You can make the fence more appealing by varying the distances between the uprights. Use several different types of wood or uneven lengths of timber for a random effect that creates an feeling of upward energy at the garden's periphery. Shape the

tops of the pickets using a jigsaw to give a rounded or pointed finish at the ends. Random pickets of long reclaimed lengths of timber can give a relaxed seaside feel. A friend of mine once adopted this method to stunning effect using reclaimed timber floorboards. A clear external wood preservative allows the beauty of the wood to show through but keeps it watertight.

Another idea is to use timber lengths horizontally, or at any angle that feels good. Setting pickets diagonally can echo the lines of the buildings surrounding you, or provide a contrast to the undulating fields of the countryside. Different widths, types and lengths of timber can be used to form a patchwork look that is strong and practical. Anything is possible as long as water is discouraged from settling on too many horizontal surfaces.

Trellis Trellis panelling is a popular timber fencing material. It is available in a wide range of patterns, diamonds and squares in softwood and hardwoods in a variety of sizes, so consider whether you want to invite attention by using diamond trellis or avoid it with laid-back squares and rectangles. Custom made trellis is now more accessible as competition increases and prices come down. Small gardens and access paths (like the side alleys in Victorian terraces) can be given depth by creating a trellis trompe l'oeil. This uses perspective to create an illusion of space. A flat background can be created by screwing lengths of marine ply to the fence posts to provide a canvas for a painted mural; simply prime it first and then get painting with exterior paint.

Marine plywood Marine plywood masking fence panels can also be used as a surface for mosaic. Alternatively, you can buy some household sticky-backed plastic (contact paper), perhaps smothered with pictures of flowers, and apply it to bring a little bit of kitsch to your garden – if you feel so inclined!

Steel & other metals If your budget allows, steel used as a solid, mesh or slatted barrier can look stunning. It can be moulded or corrugated to give a space-age, sculptural look. Stainless or galvanized steel requires little more attention than the visual demands of the onlooker, but on a large scale, sheet steel could be too dazzling on a bright, sunny day. Smaller quantities can be used to great effect: to define a seating area, in a gate or perhaps as metal railings. This makes steel and other metals much more financially attainable, too!

left: Lengths of sheet steel and cabling give a futuristic effect to a boundary clothed with the gardener's old favourite, Clematis. **above:** Metal is a versatile fencing material. This ornate screen has been left to rust and take on a deep, burnished colour that is as beautiful as the design of the fence itself. **below:** Attention to detail can be all when designing a fence. Even simple twists can add a whole new dimension. Here, the corkscrews on these iron posts point upwards to the stunning colour of the Mimosa without intruding.

THE CERAMIC GARDEN

A vibrant explosion of colour provides a breathtaking backdrop to the garden of Kaffe Fassett's London home. Much celebrated in the world of decorative arts, Kaffe's eye for colour and texture is extraordinary. Here he has tiled walls, floors and pots using a vast palette of colours, yet he manages to skilfully and successfully melt each to the next to provide a bold and imaginative display that looks ravishing even in the dead of winter.

Influenced by the Bangkok Palace Temple, Niki de Saint Phalle and Antonio Gaudi (after a visit to Parc Guell in Barcelona, Spain), amongst others, Kaffe was so inspired that he completed both terrace and walls in just three and a half days! If you feel as industrious, then remember that the secret to a successful mosaic is working with a flat surface. Employ contractors to lay a level concrete floor or to render walls, and then start looking out for tiles. Garden centres and DIY stores stock huge ranges, but scour second-hand shops as well for unusual pieces of crockery or tiles, always thinking about colour associations.

If you are covering a large area of flooring, using large pieces of tiling can result in a slippery surface so it may be wise to break tiles up into smaller fragments. Grouting will provide a more slip-resistant finish. To create more intricate designs, first mark out the design with a pencil or chalk on the level base you want to cover. When you're ready to lay the pieces, ensure that the colour combinations are grouped together. You can then use an external tile adhesive or cement-based mortar to stick your tiles down. After 2 to 3 days, when your adhesive is dry, apply grouting to the cracks. Colouring the grout with artist's pigments or acrylics can pull all the elements of a mosaic together to provide a striking display. Simply brush it on and wipe off the excess after 20 minutes. Then stand back and admire your work!

left: both floor and walls are covered in bright, textured mosaic. **below left:** close up detail of the tiling in the entrance of harlequin pattern. **below left and centre:** contrasting mosaic on the left and right of the entrance door hints at the world of colour and texture beyond, with a harlequin pattern and a gorgeous plant design. **right:** detail from the wall in the garden of a mosaic pansy. **below:** Even the plant pots have been decorated so that they complement the overall look and feel of the garden.

Iron railings and garden gates are another popular form of metal boundary, although railings are usually confined to bordering the front of the house, rather than the back garden. Nevertheless, decorative ironwork can be incorporated into more traditional boundaries such as brick walls to either provide a point through which you gain access or egress from the garden via a gate, or purely as a decorative 'hole filler' in a solid expanse of wall, to break up the solid brickwork and allow light to filter through into the garden (***see also*** Entrances and Exits, ***page 55***).

SOLID WALLING

Brick walls The brick wall is perhaps the one that we all aspire to owning. Brick exudes warmth in both colour and tone but also, physically, it harnesses the warmth of the sun's rays and acts like a radiator to plant life. It easily links the garden to the house and is useful not only for the boundary line, but for internal divisions, raised beds and retaining walls.

Choose a bond that matches the pattern in the existing brickwork of your house, topped with a simple finish. Although special bricks are produced for the top of brick walls (capping), I believe that simplicity is best, and would always use a straight soldier course. However attractive a brick wall is, the cost of such a boundary cannot be ignored. Brick is the most expensive boundary material to use; because of its small modular nature it takes a long time to lay bricks, and much of the cost in building a wall is in the skilled labour.

Rendered (plastered) concrete walls

If you want a strong solid line to divide your garden from your neighbour's, rendered walls may be an option. Concrete blocks are larger and quicker to lay than bricks, forming a surface that can be skimmed with a skin of concrete. Additives can be used to change the colour of the render, ranging from natural-looking buffs that imitate stone, through to a much stronger range of colours. Exterior masonry paint can be used to give solid blocks of colour once the render has set, or mosaic can be applied to the surface.

Drystone walling This is a traditional craft, which for many provides the accepted boundary for their property. It has rich texture, shadow and depth, which is enhanced by plants that self-seed in the cracks. They are best used in a rural setting, although I have seen an effective use of broken concrete paving slabs that emulates dry-stone walling but gives a distinctly urban feel.

Walls built without using mortar should be no more than roughly 1 metre (1 yard) in height or they can become unstable and potentially dangerous. Mortared stone can, of course, be much higher, although they still look best in a traditional rural environment.

above: Solid rendered walls can be interrupted by a cut-out, framing the tantalizing view of what lays beyond. **right:** The secret to successful drystone walling using reclaim concrete paving slabs is in keeping lines as level as possible. Use up left over slabs if you are repaving sections of your garden.

Glass blocks Another form of solid walling that creates an open feeling, allowing as much light as possible to soak into a space, is through the use of glass blocks. Textured to distort images or coloured to filter light and cast other-worldly glows,

above: Glass screens in a garden can create mood and ambience, glowing when the sun catches them. **right:** Stacked timber logs make attractive loose interior divisions, as well as creating an environment to support wildlife.

glass blocks can give a highly contemporary image to a garden, whether used at the boundary line or as interior partitions. Glass in the form of panels can make brilliantly inventive interior dividers. Coloured glass panels provide a glowing backdrop to a seating area or make an unusual boundary backdrop in a planting scheme. Pick out your favourite colour from the glass and plant up your flowerbeds to match, creating a jewel-like area of the garden. Look out for reclaimed stained-glass windows in salvage yards or commission an artist to make something for you.

INTERIOR DIVISIONS

With more and more houses being split into flats, we have to find ways to divide up a garden space for all the people who use it. The divisions need not be in the form of solid physical boundaries. Implied division, in the form of uprights, can be amazingly effective and yet still maintain an open feel.

Divisions can be temporary structures too, which makes sense if you are renting a property. In my last garden I used reclaimed copper pipe (used for plumbing), along with thick culms of bamboo salvaged from a shop refit, to split up my garden as the mood took me – running through borders one month, hiding my shed the next, supporting sweet peas and beans through the summer – and when I moved I took the piping with me.

Plots attached to new houses tend to be all the same size and if straight boundary outlines are used they will further emphasize the regularity of the space. Interior divisions in such spaces can help break up the monotony. Fence divisions (either solid or transparent) positioned at right angles to the main fence line will create movement and rhythm. This will force your garden around corners and, in turn, you'll move around your space more effectively, discovering hidden areas that will make your plot seem much bigger.

These new divisions can provide horticultural opportunities, too. For example, they can provide shelter for a nursery bed in which to grow young plants, or welcome shade for growing woodland plants. They can also create additional climbing areas, as well as simply a screened, hidden place sited away from the house where you can sit and ponder other projects in peace.

PAINT TRANSFORMATIONS

If that all sounds too much like hard work, you can always reach for the paint pot. Paint allows for one of the quickest and cheapest fence transformations possible.

And, providing your plants don't get in the way, it's easy to change your mind on the colour later!

There is a vast range of paint colours suitable for external use, or even better, use one of the new organic paints on the market that have enticing names like Tropic, Neptune and Lava, that are as vivid in colour as they are in the mind's eye. Use a shade that links to your house, perhaps the colour of your back door, gate or window frames, or the colour of your favourite plant.

In my last garden, I picked out the same shade as the large lilac tree that bowed into my space from my neighbour's garden and painted the wall that same colour. Each spring this made the whole garden appear much bigger. You could try painting different hues of the same colour on the individual pales of a closeboard fence.

Different colours can give very different effects. White can bounce light into shady areas but can tend, just like hot shades of red and orange, to become too attention-seeking, encroaching forward into a space. It is also high maintenance. Muted shades of blue and green, however, will recede, giving the effect of losing your boundary line. Spots of white paint on the fence can also be used to highlight the flowers of a favourite plant in your garden, creating halos around them. When they fade, just repaint the fence.

However, not all paint colours have to be bright and vivid. Blackboard paint can be a fun and welcome addition to a children's garden. Although it may not last very long as it is subject to fading with the sun or the rain, the surface can be easily primed and repainted when it starts to fade.

EXITS AND ENTRANCES

Pay as much attention to the entrance and exit points as you do to the rest of the space. Be they solid or see-through, they introduce the garden to your visitors. Choose a complementary or contrasting material to your boundary line but, if you can afford it, buy a beautiful gate. A gate splits up areas within the garden, resulting in it appearing much bigger; a sense of mystery is conjured up by a gate that makes visitors yearn to see what's behind. Whatever your final decision, your boundary should have personality; it should fit in with your garden and the surrounding environment and, most of all, with you. When it comes to fences and walls, I believe we should all be stretching the boundaries.

Metalwork doesn't have to be utilitarian, as this gate illustrates. It can be unstructured, delicate and graceful.

STRUCTURES

All too often the importance of vertical accents in the garden in the form of structures is overlooked; simple arches are thrown into a space as an afterthought. But, when thrusting skywards, arches, pergolas, arbours, obelisks, summerhouses and gazebos create uplift in the garden, taking the eye away from the ground to go up and through the space. Structures add tension, ambience, movement and mystery to a space – all welcome additions. Vertical structures create the ceiling of the garden, and if you use complementary or contrasting materials, they really make the garden become an outdoor room.

Garden structures can give a feeling of protection; somehow it is much easier to relax outside on your deckchair when you are in or near a structure such as a gazebo, summerhouse or even just an awning, than when you are out in an open position.

PERGOLAS

Pergolas are appealing vertical structures in any garden, inviting exploration and movement. Architecturally, pergolas can have a strong impact and, if the siting has been well considered, they can create a play with light and shade to cast some amazing shadows. As long as thought has been given to the placing of the horizontals, and the plants trained to clothe it, building a pergola can be a great way of providing pleasant solitude with a good amount of light in a very built-up space.

Siting A pergola creates a good overhead transition between the house and the garden. They are bridging structures, linking elements to be used in conjunction with other landscaping features to lead you through a space. In hot climates they are likely to stretch along a network of paths to provide protection from the sun, but they can work equally well in short bursts, covering only part of the path to create a feeling of weaving in and out, even on the straightest of routes. In urban areas where houses are neatly filed side-by-side, a pergola fixed to the back of the house creates not just shade but a degree of privacy, too.

Pergolas must be well situated so that they do not look out of place with their surroundings. A pergola placed in the middle of a garden for no apparent reason will just look wrong.

above and right: Whether you choose a garden pergola that is slick, cool and contemporary, or solid and more traditional, this type of structure will lift your eye, creating an upward sweep in hard landscaping and your garden.

Proportions The proportions of the pergola are of paramount importance for making the whole visual effect work – and they are excruciatingly difficult to get right. Too often the vertical posts that hold the overhead horizontals are too large, making the horizontals look flimsy and the whole structure somehow unbalanced. It is also difficult to achieve the right proportion between height, width and length.

Draw up your ideas then mark them out on the ground to ensure that your structure doesn't become oppressive. An imagined stroll through a pergola that frames leafy views of the garden can easily change a pleasant walk into a dash down an overbearing, constricting tunnel once you have done it for real. Generally, the more generous the scale the better.

Design Pick out architectural details in your house to help with the design of your construction. Echoing the height of doors, roofs or window tops, as well as the materials used, will gel the divide

between house and garden. Dimensions and pre-planning are king here. As a general rule of thumb, leave about 50cm (20in) clear of an adult's height for the height of your upright verticals. The horizontals that mark the width should be wide enough to allow two people to walk through comfortably side-by-side.

It may seem obvious, but remember that pergolas don't have to be straight. A curve can be more gentle on the eye and will encourage investigation, as whatever is at the end of the covered walk will not be immediately obvious. A journey through a pergola can be very different, depending on the construction of its frame. Windows into the garden can be made if the sides have some more closed areas, framing different views as you walk down its length. When used to frame a path, pergolas can become a series of unconnected arches or frames, or they can become continuous tunnels.

Remember, too, that the pergola should look good from all angles. It should look as attractive from the upstairs window as it does from the ground, and it should be pleasing to the eye when walking through it and when viewing it from the garden.

Great uneven lengths of soaring uprights can suggest a pergola design, but by omitting the horizontals that usually brace the top of the structure, it will leave the sky free of visual disturbance, allowing you to see sky, clouds and birds.

Materials Pergolas don't have to be constructed from timber. Think about the mood of the garden and the period of the house or garden surrounding your envisioned path framework. Brick, rendered columns, metal, trellising, wire or even glass can be stunning materials to use (provided they fit into the overall scheme).

Consider also plants that you might wish to grow up them; is your pergola an architectural framework to simply stroll under, or is it a tool to enable you to grow plants up into a different dimension? If the first is the case, then use a dramatic material or over-sized proportions to make the structure sculptural. If the latter is the case, your structure should incorporate strength as well as support to hold the weight of climbing plants.

A pergola need not be permanent. Copper pipe or bamboo canes sunk into the earth, or held in place in pots filled with sand or gravel, can be lashed together with garden twine or wire to provide a temporary structure that you can move wherever you like.

TUNNELS

When a pergola has no point of exit throughout its length except when you reach the very end of its run, it becomes an exciting, mysterious tunnel. This type of tunnel works best if its proportions are generous, with enough light to filter through to become dappled and shady, but not dismal.

If the dimensions are too small, a tunnel can become oppressive, threatening and dark; hardly enjoyable to walk through! However, this is not necessarily true for children, who generally like nothing better than to squeeze their way through a tight, restricting play tunnel.

left: Structurally independent, these plastic-coated arches are brought together visually by a thick clothing of plants. Garden structures certainly open another arena for displaying plants, as well as bringing a sculptural quality to garden landscaping. **below:** Pliable natural materials such as willow, bamboo and hazel can be bent into shapes and forms to create spectacular but informal garden structures.

THREE DIMENSIONAL

If you're brave, hard landscaping materials can dominate a space, giving the garden an upward surge of energy. Here, rendered (plastered) block walls become pure sculpture, giving the garden architectural strength and a firm footing throughout the seasons. The free-form walling also creates depth and altered perspective, making the boundaries of the garden completely blurred as the eye is drawn into the centre.

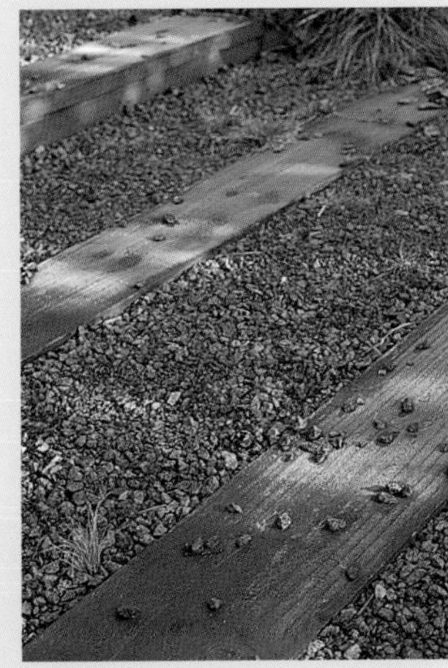

The rendered block walls within the space create loose garden compartments. Where the walls bisect each other, new angles and corners are created away from the garden's boundary walls. These new junctions draw the eye towards the planting within. This effect could prove heavy and dominating, but due to large cut-out holes and smaller geometric apertures that pierce the walls themselves, light is allowed to shaft through. These spaces invite the user to see what lies beyond them; they frame other compartments and highlight plants that are in full bloom, making the garden visually stunning. Such boldness is to be encouraged.

The designer of this space, Bonita Bulaitis, has no fear of pronounced architectural lines, strong hard landscaping features and intense colour. The garden is stimulating because every inch of hard landscaping within the whole has been carefully considered and artfully introduced. Half-hearted attempts always look weak. If you're going to commit to something, then go the whole distance. If at first your landscape detailing looks hard and cold, with a little forethought you can make the planting soften its edges. The planting in this garden balances the design as a whole. Grasses glide through the space, softening hard edges and blurring lines. The internal divisions form a backdrop to more solid plantings of trees and shrubs.

Underfoot, the landscaping is softer, too. Chipped stone crunches loose beneath your feet, awakening senses other than sight. Sunken railway sleepers (ties) have an earthiness in delicious contrast to the Modernism of the concrete structures. Laid across the path, and so the line of vision, they slow you down as you walk through the space, inviting you to linger and explore what lies around them.

Internal divisions and structures are invaluable to a space, making it appear larger by inviting exploration. Here they are bonded into the earth, sunk deep below the ground's surface, as if to stake their claim in belonging to the space. There is no doubt in my mind that they definitely do.

far left top: This three-dimensional space uses vertical and horizontal space to the maximum to create a garden that has many well-considered layers. **far left middle:** Planting not only softens the lines of structures but also highlights architectural detail. **far left bottom:** This Perspex water fountain looks attractive even when the water is not running. Here in the early morning frost it glistens in the sunlight. **top left:** Railway sleepers (ties) slow down the garden user's pace when laid across a path's direction of movement. **middle left:** Holes cut from the rendered walls accentuate views and vistas, drawing attention to the open garden compartments that lie beyond. **left:** Bisecting internal dividers create corners from which the planting flows out. This provides an illusion of space, even in the tiniest of gardens. **above**: The early morning frost on sleepers melts away slowly, focusing attention on the wood's deep grain.

Any material can be used to make a tunnel, but choosing plants and materials that are derived from natural origins seem to work best. Trees, traditionally beech, yew or lime, can be trained so that they arch upwards to meet at the top, but you will need patience for the trees to reach their desired height. Willow or bamboo can be woven together to make architectural tunnels that become large-scale sculptures. The snaking yew tunnel at Trevarno in Cornwall, England is a good example of this.

ARBOURS, GAZEBOS AND SUMMERHOUSES

Traditionally, arbours were built as shady retreats sited amongst the trees, although now they are used mainly as structural features to grow plants up, often positioned against a wall and with a seat or bench beneath the framework structure. The dictionary definition of a gazebo is 'a garden summerhouse or pavilion sited to command a good view'. Today we easily interchange these terms, in essence using either to refer to garden structures (be they open or closed) that provide shade and shelter from the sun and wind.

above, right and below: Garden structures can really make or break a garden's style, much more so than other hard landscaping components. Style is distinguished not only by the application of design but also in the construction detailing. Think carefully about the look you want to achieve in your space.

There are lots of types of pre-fabricated structures on the market. When thinking about buying a gazebo, all you need is space to put it. They are formed from many different materials. Wood is perhaps the cheapest, and can be painted or stained as you prefer. If the shelter is close to the house, however, the structure looks best if it matches or complements the building through the use of similar materials.

Usually, though, such structures are often completely secluded, and so can be treated entirely individually. Simple structures made from rustic materials can look fantastic in garden settings. Jill Smallcombe builds summerhouses with cob (a mixture of subsoil, water and straw) that appear to have erupted from the very earth that they are made from. Matt Rant, a hazel and willow weaver, manipulates withies to form open, light, gentle arbours, that will continue evolving and growing for many years after they they were first erected.

A summerhouse does not need to be ornate or fancy. A simple, roofed shelter that provides shade and seclusion away from the house is ripe for the development of a personal style. It also does not have to be constructed from simple materials. Live in Art produce sophisticated polyurethane installations with elegant archways, which although stunningly modern, have an organic form that ensures that the structures sit comfortably in the garden environment.

Where there are walls or fences in your garden, you may be able to use these to partially support a gazebo or a roof canopy of some kind. Overhead structures certainly don't have to be freestanding.

AWNINGS

Where two walls meet in a corner, overhead beams or awnings are easily installed. Awnings can be made to measure, then simply rolled out from fittings attached to a wall. Alternatively, they can be far more relaxed in style, comprising little more than a sheet strung from branches, poles or posts. Sail fabric, stretching tight from walls or fences, can look very effective and casts shade well. Whether they are professionally fitted or home-made, awnings make exciting temporary structures, providing useful shade from strong sun.

Awnings can transform a space quickly and effectively. The loose sail fabric used in the awning shown here is suspended from a scaffold pole; simple, but very effective – and it would be very easy to reproduce.

SHEDS AND STORES

Another form of shelter, traditionally used as storage for tools and gardening sundries, is the garden shed. This is usually hidden behind screens, and tucked away into the back of the garden. But when space is limited, and most gardens are too small to hide buildings in, there has been a backlash against hiding such useful, hardworking items.

Sheds have become multi-functional, and are now embraced and celebrated through decoration and adornment. Tools are often the last things you find in a shed – they are increasingly more often used as a home office, playroom – or even a bar!

Metal chemical stores or cabinets can be purchased to store tools and materials in giving a modern high-tech twist to the traditional timber shed. Lean-to sheds are useful for small spaces, as they can be tucked away in side alleys to the house or in corners of the garden.

OBELISKS

Not all garden structures are in the form of garden buildings. Obelisks are tall needle-shaped structures that have been used for garden ornament since ancient Egyptian times.

Used in a variety of ways throughout garden history, they remain one of the most familiar shapes in the garden today, either purely as an ornamental feature or as a structure upon which to train climbing plants. Available in timber, metal, stone or topiarized yew, box or bay, all of them provide a welcome exclamation mark to any garden space. Used in front of an entrance or at the start of a path, they emphasise the importance of such a beginning.

above: Treated in a contemporary way, this chunky timber bridge provides such a feeling of movement that it looks as if it needs its timber pins to hold it down! **left:** With its graceful curve and unusual tiled surface, this simple, sleek bridge would look at home in both an urban or rural environment.

BRIDGES

Used to traverse streams, pools or rivers, bridges can also cross planting borders or dry riverbeds of gravel and stone. They provide a different level to view the garden, giving a new perspective. You can use bridges to connect the different elements of 'vertical' gardens that are formed on many different levels – it seems a shame to use them only for watery environments.

ORNAMENT

Ornaments are the accessories to any garden. If chosen sensitively, garden ornament can capture the spirit of a place and provide the decorative accents that pull the whole scheme together. However, an ornament can just as easily shatter a garden's harmony. An inappropriate piece can splinter the cohesion and unity of a space; does a Victorian piece of cast-iron ornament work within a sleek contemporary setting? Not really but, strangely, the opposite seems to work: a modern piece can look visually stunning in a traditional garden space.

When you think about garden ornament, the first things that spring to mind are a piece of sculpture or ornamental urns, but furniture, obelisks, plant supports and the 'sculpted' plants themselves are all active in setting the garden scene. They are so important that it may sometimes be necessary to adjust your hard landscaping to incorporate a particularly welcome piece. Garden accessories are used foremost as garden focal points at the end of vistas or to lead the eye around the garden to accentuate a good view (or detract from a horrible one).

However, it is important to remember that sometimes tension can be heightened in the garden by the lack of a focal point where one might expect to see one, and this can become a very powerful statement. A classic example of this is at the end of a garden where a path leads out into the open fields beyond. Placing any kind of ornamental feature would stop the flow of the eye and lose the benefit of the borrowed view beyond.

SCULPTURE

Modern garden sculpture is at last becoming more acceptable within the garden space. It has been difficult in the past to obtain good pieces due to the lack of public demand. People have associated the buying of

Sculpture can be combined to be not only attractive but also practical. Here in the Prince's Trust Garden at Chelsea 2000, the copper spiral structure catches rainwater and channels it into the pool below.

above and below: Terri Pickup's work often uses the ancient process of lost waxing casting to produce sculpture and vessels that imitate natural forms. The coral-like garden ornament is glass. The urn is made using the same process but in aluminium and bronze.

pieces purely to add decorative interest to a garden as pretentious and extravagant, but due to heightened interest in the garden environment, it is now becoming acceptable.

Most of us want the garden to be as beautiful as it possibly can be. If embellishing a space with one, or several, key pieces is appropriate and suits us, the gardeners, it seems absurd not to go ahead and buy something that will add the final polish to a garden that has been well thought out.

Sculpture has an all-season presence, giving permanence and vitality to the garden when herbaceous plants have gone for the winter. It can evolve into an indispensable piece, even when affected by the weather. The ageing effects of wind, snow, frost and rain result in the feeling that a sculpture has evolved from the environment itself.

Sculpture today can be bought off-the-rack, commissioned, or made oneself by utilizing found pieces. It can be practical or purely aesthetic. It can dominate an area, or be very subtle. Sculpture can create impact or emphasize a key area of planting. Buy whatever you like, but remember to keep the desired feature in scale with the rest of the garden – you don't want any piece to be overpowering. However, being too cautious can result in lots of bitty, unrelated small pieces that clutter up an area, resulting in it becoming insignificant as a whole. Grouping pieces together works best if they have an overall thread or linking style to bind them together: perhaps they are by the same artist, constructed using the same material, or have a uniting theme. If unsure, it is best to commit to a piece, invest wisely and place different sculptures in situations where they can be given the space to be viewed and enjoyed individually on their own merits, without interference by another piece.

This is not to say that placing sculpture against a positive backdrop of hard or soft landscaping does not work. A brightly coloured wall or distinguished yew hedge can work as a frame and highlight a piece, adding depth and resonance to a strong background where the piece can bask at the end of a clean view. Sculpture enclosed by a throng of foliage, or an architectural chair invitingly placed in the middle of a meadow or flower border, can be allowed to glow quietly in its surroundings.

You can create sculptural pieces yourself at home using almost any material imaginable. Allow the mind to run wild when considering construction, finish and surface texture and you'll achieve some amazing results.

Wood I have long had a love affair with timber. To me, wood seems to have a warmth and depth that is a welcome addition in any space. Carved wood reliefs can be placed on walls; planed, treated pieces can rise from the earth whence it originally came, adding a fragile permanency that is delicate and refined.

It is wood in the raw that I really embrace: reclaimed hulks of twisted tree trunks or elegantly bound bunches of twigs seem to reinforce the relationship with the living, growing surroundings that the gardener works with on a day-to-day basis. Even hazel twigs used as plant supports become practical sculptural pieces that seem to evoke times past simply by being there. Upright sleepers, or ties, positioned so that they are pointing skywards, sweep the garden upwards into the air.

Sandblasted, or gathered from the seashore, wood is a very evocative material when it is moulded by the elements. It can be used to create magnificent sculptural arrangements. If you are handy with a chainsaw then the connotations are endless.

Steffi Thomas of Vivid Space uses reclaim railway sleepers (ties) to produce soft, warm and friendly decorative garden structures.

THE ARTIST'S GARDEN

In their garden at the edge of a forest in the Rhine Valley, Germany, artist Siegfried Speckhardt and his wife Ri, have created a wonderful otherworld. The garden is a canvas for installations, buildings and sculpture that create exciting visuals and inspired hard landscaping effects. Siegried uses materials around him to create features that effortlessly blend into the garden as a whole. The 'found' materials come first, then the ideas follow...

On a trip around the garden you encounter reclaim bridges created from odds and ends of metal held in place with twisted pieces of timber. Sculptures nestling in undergrowth are pieced together with parts from old sewing machines. Sudden bursts of painted bright colour transform objects from bland to beautiful with a brushstroke. It's a garden bursting at the seams with creativity and unusual ideas put together on a shoestring, whilst still creating maximum impact.

Everyday items seem highlighted, fresh and new in this artistic environment. Even the yard where wood is stored has impact. Although first and foremost it is a productive outdoor

above left: The wood storeyard seems to be the creative hub of the garden. Full of texture and shape, the scene is constantly changing as wood is used. **below left:** Industrial scrap, welded into position, forms the gate that holds the garden within. The finished effect is practical but doesn't take itself too seriously. I just love the spanner gate latch! **left:** Spray-painted industrial hose sweeps head over heels to create a robust spiral sculpture. It injects movement and vitality to the garden as it tumbles down a slope. **right:** The original owner has cast these sheet steel templates aside, yet the magpie in Siegfried stores them for a rainy day. **below:** Blue is Siegried's central motif; he's used the colour in much of his work. The Blue Temple is certainly the central focal point of the garden and seems to watch sentry-like over the rest of the space. Within it's construction, several contrasting and complementary materials are used, yet the paint draws them all together.

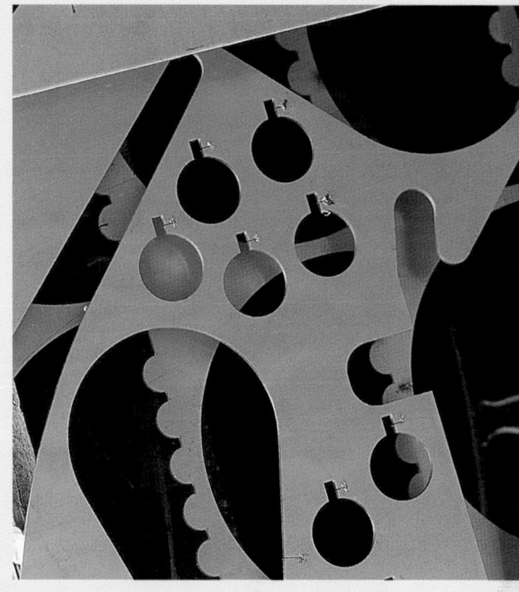

storeroom, the atmosphere of the area seems almost celebratory; chunks of wood are strewn or randomly stacked and invite you to reach out and touch. Nothing seems to be thrown away for fear that it could be useful at some time for some thing. The Speckhardt's garden is, in places, a tantalizing storage space for ideas that are sure to come to the owners later.

The finished effect of a garden created in this way is a space that brims with originality and the owners' personalities. Arbours and walkways created from reclaim objects hold memories of the places and times the materials came from, the processes used in putting them together, and of course, the many happy days and hours spent enjoying building and using them in the garden itself.

If, like me, you are forever collecting bits and pieces from here and there, then providing you have the space, the skies the limit to what you can create. If not, then you'll need to look out for visually interesting textures and materials and grab them while you can. Keep objects that call out to you, even if you're not sure what you will eventually use them for – or one day you might regret it!

above: Wood can be shaped and turned to make highly individual pieces of garden ornamentation. **right:** Pieces of stone, quarried from the earth and positioned in a spot that shows them to their full advantage, can be highly effective.

Cast concrete Reproduction statutory produced in concrete is finding its feet in contemporary landscape design. Garden centres are now stocked with more adventurous pieces which, due to advanced production methods, weather much more satisfactorily than they have in the past. It is cheaper than stone, so it can well be worth hunting down that elusive perfect piece.

Contrary to popular belief, concrete is a very pliable material and can be moulded into fantastical shapes to form the basis of amazing mosaics. If this sounds a little too ambitious, grab some pre-made concrete statutory, then apply mosaic to its surface to produce transformations of your own.

Terracotta For long confined to the plant container, clay sculpture is being produced today by more avant-garde potters which is not quite so obvious. Ceramic mobiles placed in trees tremble in the breeze, creating music that seems to fall from the air around you. Clay, ranging in colour from deep red to light biscuit, is easily moulded into almost anything you want it to be, such as candlesticks or chandeliers to light your garden evenings. Jonathon Garret produces 'garden punctuations' consisting of earthenware arrows at the end of long poles to shock, surprise and inject humour. Coloured glazes can produce a myriad of tones to complement or contrast, as you see fit.

Stone Monolithic dolmens when used as standing stones are sculptural in the raw. With a wide range of colour and finishes, stone can be exploited in the garden to produce pieces that are tactile, cool and refreshing. Stone is a versatile material that can be placed around the garden to attract, surprise or just to 'be'.

Statuary, obelisks and wall plaques around the world have been hewn from great hunks of stone for centuries, but contemporary work using the same materials can be just as spectacular. Will and Lottie O'Leary are masters of stonemasonry, creating carved pieces and slabs of lettering that give a modern edge to a traditional craft. Last time I visited them, Lottie was carving an enormous lobster from a piece of Welsh stone, proving that anything is possible with a little imagination.

Metals If left to its own devices, metals such as steel, iron and copper will deteriorate at the whim of the natural processes activated by all the elements. With time, rain, salty air, frost and snow mould the surface of such materials, creating sculptural pieces that are full of character and personality. Rust brings with it hues that are so readily associated with the earth: ochres, reds, and browns, giving an air of fragility to what will in fact be solid structures for years to come.

Incorporating metals into your garden may be as simple as using some aluminium spirals piercing through the foliage of a plant.

If you find this natural erosion appealing, but simply don't have the patience to wait for it to occur, there are those out there that will speed up the process for you. More and more designers are embracing the oxidization process to give mild steel a new lease of life. An artist I know uses this technique to celebrate rust in his obelisks, urns and armillary spheres, which, if positioned sensitively, look stunning when pierced by shafts of light. James Price, a sculptor working in the southern coastal climes of Brighton, weaves ordinary fencing wire into extraordinary vessels and sprays them with salt water, leaving it to time to turn them all shades of fiery orange.

If the appeal of rust does not sneak into your aesthetic palette, metals can be moulded into great sweeps of work. Blacksmiths are now producing great curvy pieces that encompass all that is natural. Metals are moulded with infinite delicacy into rolling pieces of fencing, gates, fountains and arbours that have come a long way from the great balls of fire from which they were produced.

If you would like to try your hand at making something quite magical from metals, go ahead; you might create something exquisite. In my last garden I used copper piping to create drifts of golden uprights, which quickly streaked with green corrosion, to create rhythm and movement in my dowdy winter borders.

Plants Although not perhaps at first associated with sculpture, plants can be manipulated through topiary, which is an art form in itself. If you do not have the time to be clipping the shapes of animals and birds into your yew, a more geometric shape, such as a cone or ball, is a more manageable option.

Willow can also be woven into incredible forms, which live and grow in the same way. Love it or hate it, training living materials into shapes and spires produces some other-worldly results, as can be seen at Bonfante Gardens in California.

URNS AND CONTAINERS

There is always a place in any garden for a pot, be it as an architectural addition or as a receptacle for a plant. Available in a vast range of materials, such as wood, stone, terracotta, metal, plastic or wire, if placed with thought they can punctuate the

above left: Custom made reflective metal vessels look ultra-modern and slick – and don't have to contain plants! **above right:** A metal bin is left outside to rust, taking on the hues of the grass it holds. **above far right:** Containers are a useful way of adding colour to a garden. Move brightly coloured urns through your borders to give them a lift and to fill in empty spaces. **left:** Terracotta is now taking on chic new shapes to meet modern garden trends and fashions.

garden journey. Urns and containers look great when grouped together in clusters of vibrant colour, achieved through the containers themselves or the plants that they contain.

However, they don't have to be confined to ground level. Wall-mounted window boxes or hanging containers can ease the transition from house to garden, in fact, any vertical surface can be home to a planting vessel. Mounted high on the boundary fence of a garden, lightweight plastic containers rammed with trailing ivy allude to great sweeping curtains of leaf in a garden that I have designed. Braced to the top of a shed roof, climbers can flow in a free-form fashion down the sides in a great waterfall of foliage and flower.

Display your containers on a tiered stand to really show off your prize petunias and maximize space. Line them up at the edge of steps or patios to act as full stops or semi-permanent dividers that can be moved around as the mood takes you.

Containers are there to have fun with. Anything can potentially be a plant pot: old sinks, buckets, tin cans, heating ducts, even the boot of an old car can inject humour and personality into a space. Recycle old plant pots with paint, dress them with twigs, rope or mosaic, or spray them with Hammerite, or something similar, to give them a metallic sheen.

OUTDOOR FURNITURE

What would a garden be without somewhere to sit and admire the view? Outdoor furniture is becoming more and more inventive as the gardening boom develops. Designs range from the traditional through reproduction to the modern; they can be either very simple or highly complex in construction to give a multitude of effects. Seating can be free-standing, allowing it to be moved, or it can be built into your hard landscaping, although this is obviously not as versatile. Although it may seem obvious, remember that other hard landscaping features such as steps, low walls, raised decks or jetties over water can all be comfortable and convenient places to sit.

Some pieces of furniture can be multifunctional, too. I have a blue reinforced fibreglass Phantom chair designed by Verner Panton that works well as a seat, a chaise longue, a bench and a table; with the limited space in my garden, this works extremely well.

Comfort is paramount when buying furniture. Aways try before you buy, and bear in mind that a stunningly designed piece with a high price tag does not always ensure comfort! Different materials used in construction can have advantages and disadvantages that should be considered, too.

Timber Perhaps the most versatile of materials for outdoor furniture, there is a vast range of wood types ranging from iroko to teak, all with very distinct qualities. Timber can be planed to perfection to give a timeless quality piece, or it can be more rustic in construction. Even a felled tree trunk can be a convenient, comfortable perch for a while. Remember that hardwoods have more longevity than softwoods, and that there are countless styles available; research is a must in order to eliminate your options.

Metal and plastics Metals can be very uncomfortable and cold to the touch. Ranging from the traditional cast-iron seats and

Seats with personality can add a much-needed injection of fun to a space. Look out in shops specialising in interiors for seats and chairs that could easily make the transition outside.

tables produced for Victorian gardens through the lighter, more comfortable and less expensive aluminium alloys, to stainless steel and aluminium (which can cost a fortune), metal looks so attractive that it would be a shame not to add it as the icing on the cake in a high-tech garden.

Plastics, reinforced fibre-glass and plastic-coated furniture are a much more affordable and practical option.

Wipe-clean, very light and versatile, they are available in a range of bright colours. However, ensure that they are treated with UV inhibitors so they don't fade or become unstable when exposed to sunlight. Because of their reasonable cost, you can replace them with less guilt than you can with a high-tech designer item!

below: A solid timber seat will always be desirable in the garden. Dependable and timeless, look out for chairs in the same timber as your deck, or with lines that echo other garden architecture.

right: Perspex furniture is light and easy to clean. Here, transparent seats bring a space bang up to date.

STONE, CONCRETE AND CERAMIC

Stone is incredibly heavy, making it more suitable for permanent installations in the garden. There is something deeply romantic about a potting table constructed from a great slab of slate.

Concrete can also be very heavy, but it can be used to unusual sculptural effect. Dan Pearson's practical, low concrete wall seating in a London restaurant garden is effective through its simplicity. More eloquent is Willy Guhl's Luke rocking chair

constructed from reinforced concrete; uncompromisingly stylish, it is surprisingly comfortable to sit on (see page 168).

Used to provide similar effects to concrete, ceramics are becoming increasingly popular, taking the form of simple stools and low benches right through to the extraordinarily elaborate ceramic throne made by Emma Lush.

LIVING SEATS

A raised seat created in turf, chamomile, box or willow gives the traditional cottage garden a contemporary slant; just don't wear your favourite trousers when you want to sit down!

To make a living seat, construct a hollow frame using hazel, willow, timber or any other material that takes your fancy. Fill the void with soil until full, incorporating plenty of gravel for drainage. Then simply lay turves or low-growing herbs such as thyme or chamomile to create an organic, living seat. Feed it regularly until established and give it a clip when it needs it.

Trees have been grafted to make bizarre shapes in seats that amaze some, but that I personally can't abide – they remind me of Japanese foot binding, which seems to me to be more tree torture than tree liberating.

Garden ornaments can replace plants altogether in some areas of the garden, providing the ultimate low-maintenance option!

HAMMOCK

The most indispensable item, which I personally can't do without, is a hammock. Lying in a Mexican string hammock on a warm summer's evening is the ultimate in luxury! If you don't have two trees conveniently set apart from which to sling it, then there are free-standing hammock frames available, or you could set two posts into the ground with concrete to act as supports. Grow plants up to disguise the posts, then swing away to your heart's content.

WATER

Cooling, soothing and refreshing, water is a highly emotive addition to any garden hard landscaping. Ever-changing and effervescent, water is the most flexible element that can be used in a garden. With its wide-ranging applications, it has become one of the most fashionable features in the garden today.

Most of us do not have the space, time, money or desire to build anything like the elaborate waterscapes that were achieved on the grand estates built during the Renaissance and Romantic periods, but we can be inspired by them. We can also make our own interpretations of these schemes and incorporate these ideas into the hard landscaping of a garden, which will provide the foundation of surprisingly fresh schemes.

The size of your garden will probably affect your choice of water feature more than any other hard landscaping material decisions. Water feature choices are vast, ranging from a calm mist of water droplets through to pools of reflective stillness or the excitement of crashing white waterfalls. All will affect a site dramatically, so choose with care, taking as much time as possible before you make your decision.

PLACEMENT

Perhaps the first consideration should be where you will place your feature. If your garden is close to a busy road, there is nothing like the gentle splash of a small fountain of moving water to detract from it, but if it becomes an overpowering roar

left: Adding personality to a garden is extremely important, and this eccentric zip water feature does just that! **above:** Allison Armour-Wilson's aquasphere appears to float over a concave pool of stainless steel. It seems to encapsulate many of the qualities that makes water so special in a garden; it is cooling, tranquil and refreshing. **opposite:** Reflection is another element that still water has, not just reflecting the sky, plants or buildings, but water itself.

close to a seating area, the noise could become too much and be annoying, rather than calming and relaxing.

Moving water has another dimension that is sometimes overlooked – light. Placing a fountain, jet or cascade in a spot where natural light can refract through it can provide glistening, effervescent effects.

Where water occurs naturally in heavy clay soils, you can encourage a pond to form by excavating a bowl for the water to collect in, or digging a channel for a stream to run along. But, be aware that if you put in anything more permanent it could cause problems, as water will have its own way: the natural water beneath it could lift a rigid pool out; it could be flooded; or, if concrete is used, the walls could crack.

When considering placement, there are a few more considerations to ponder. Although a pool in a leafy glade surrounded

scape. Hand-chosen, weathered sculptural rocks glide through the gravel, reminiscent of mountains surrounding the sea. Pebbles are strewn beach-like to surround the smaller gravelly waters enclosed within, and hunks of rock stand sentry, overseeing the space as a whole.

The garden is ordered and yet has a spirit of the natural; larger stones are selected and placed at the feet of the Agaves that puncture the beach-like gravel to imitate water drops falling from their spiny leaves. Reminiscent of Zen gardening, everything has its place, its meaning and its purpose. As a result the gardens, though contemplative and restful, lock rhythm, movement and energy into their core. They are challenging and exciting; you can't bear to take your eyes away for a moment, just in case you miss something

above left: Swirls of raked gravel are surrounded by mounds of planting, while flat planes of grass and monolithic wedges of stone echo a watery otherworld. **below left:** A detail of the cobbles used to imitate the ripples of water. **left:** Like the scales on a dragon's back, a stacked slate river provides a textural contrast to the other materials used in the space **below:** Surfacing does not have to invite you to walk upon it, and here, garden flooring has been used in such a way that it is purely aesthetic. **right:** Raked gravel is quintessentially karesansui, the Japanese art of dry landscaping, and evokes the spirit of calming water.

Small-scale water features If you simply don't have the space for a large pool, pond, stream or rill, a water feature is not impossible. However small your garden, there will be a feature that is suitable for you. Remember, where there's a will, there's a way!

Small-garden owners will probably have already realized the importance of maximizing the space in a garden by utilizing vertical expanses, and garden walls are the perfect way to get water into your space. The back of your house is the ideal spot if you are not so lucky as to have a walled boundary line. This also has the benefit of drawing the garden-user out of the house to unravel the mystery of where the gurgling sound of water is coming from.

All too often, water features are placed opposite a door or window leading into the garden, which offers no surprises, and actually tends to make a garden seem smaller. If you have arranged the garden in this way, the whole space is just too obvious to the user – what's the point in going outside if you can see everything from the kitchen window?

Wall fountains Wall fountains are arranged in much the same way as a pool and fountain, but here a submersible pump, housed in a waterproof container, pushes water up through a pipe to surge through an opening further up the wall. There are lots of wall-fountain kits available through gardening retail outlets, but with a little imagination, a customized wall-mounted feature can be much more stunning. Recycled objects, such as a watering can or an old tap, or a contemporary sculpture, can be used to add your own twist to a well-used effect.

Miniature ponds The simplest and quickest way to get water into your garden is almost too obvious. Remember that any waterproof vessel can be transformed into a miniature pond; the only limits here are budget and vision.

WATER SAFETY

One of the overriding considerations when thinking about using water in a family garden is the safety of young children. They, too, are mesmerized by water and this attraction can be dangerous. However, you do not need to rule out the inclusion of water simply because you have a young family. Securely fix a safety mesh just under the water surface, so that if a child were to fall in, the depth of the water is at a minimum. Smaller children should never be left unattended in a garden, with or without water. However, there are even safer options.

Bubble fountains One of the safest water features is a bubble fountain. The water reservoir is hidden beneath a grate covered in pebbles, and the water trickles out over the surface of a large rock or millstone. The conventional construction technique can be adapted to incorporate glass beads or coloured gravel as the reservoir covering, providing a shimmering effervescence that is enhanced by the flow of water over it. Any type of piping, stone or decorative container can be drilled through to provide an exit point for water to flow from and over. Experimentation can prove satisfyingly successful.

CHILD'S PLAY

Safety is of course paramount, but there are many practical and safe solutions that can add infinite amounts of fun into the family space, and children love to play in water. Hard surfacing can be punctuated with play jets which shoot up through the ground to provide a refreshing soak in summer. Troughs and sinks can be arranged so they are at the right height for small hands to play in, but impossible for a child to fall into.

A fantastic paddling stream has been designed by Roger Storr, which, when filled with water, forms a shallow channel to play in until the water dries out.

WALKING ON WATER

There is a wealth of water-garden accessories and features that will support and enhance your whole scheme. Navigating your way up, over and through your waterscape should be one of the first considerations when planning your hardscape scheme.

Stepping stones These are a fantastic way to traverse your waterways. Laid slightly higher than the water or just skimming its surface, they slow down your pace, allowing you the time to view what lies both around and below you. A vast range of materials can be used, providing they give a non-slip surface to walk on. This can be stone, timber, glass, brick or logs, as they can all add to a given effect.

Play with the proportions to provide larger areas in the run where one can rest a while, and experiment with the direction that they are laid in. Stepping stones can randomly

Islands within pools give a peaceful, restful feel. If you were alone sitting on this isle, I'm sure you'd feel calm and relaxed, even though the reflections of the surrounding buildings show that in reality, you wouldn't be.

meander across the water or confidently span directly across a width, adding different resonance to a scene.

Bridges Bridges provide a more stable option than stepping stones and can be just as simple to construct. Easier, cheaper and no less effective, a few planks of wood or a large sheet of stone is an effective way to cross water, detracting nothing from the watery scene. Expanding on this idea, a timber boardwalk leading out from the bank, without a handrail and with the planks laid in the same direction as the water's flow, encourages the eye to stay low and view the plants, insects and fish either in or on the water itself.

But this simple type of construction would be inappropriate for a more formal style. Wood, stone or metal bridges can be as elaborate or as uncomplicated as you wish. By the very nature of their shape and scale, they will be more prominent that a water-skimming boardwalk. This can be put to good use if you allow the imagination full rein to create a breathtaking focal point as well as a practical means of crossing.

WATER MARGINS

The edges of any type of pool or stream deserve your attention, in both decorative and functional treatments. Well-placed statuary meandering down a stream can pepper its edges, creating a rhythm that moves the vision ever forward in anticipation of the next piece of eye-candy. Mirrors used at the water's edge, perhaps on a wall, create the illusion that the water goes on into the distance, which could be perfect for the smaller space.

Beaches At the edge of a pool a bank of pebbles or recycled crushed glass can provide a small beach to enable the user to get close to the water, allowing them to reach out and make contact with the water more easily. In my experience, it's nigh on impossible to resist paddling in a pond that has the added invitation of a beach! A gentle slope or plank at the edge of a pool will also help the wildlife that uses the pool, too – that is, if you want them to.

Surface materials The areas adjacent to pools and ponds should be considered at the same time as choosing your water feature. Materials reaching into a pond to create rivulets or islands can look stunning. Decks are brilliant for this purpose as they have the sublime added benefit of allowing you to dangle your feet into the water. Wood and water are just a perfect combination to have.

LIGHTING

Lighting is an important aspect to consider when planning serious hard landscaping. After all, this is the obvious time to get your armoured cable laid to make lighting the garden easier once it's finished. When installing lighting it is always sensible to employ a professional to do the electrical work – a local contractor may be all you need. However, employing a professional lighting designer or lighting company may show you how to maximize your budget to create a more interesting and innovative scheme.

These rippling lights in my own garden were made by wrapping cheap exterior lighting around lengths of bent metal. They show that interesting lighting need not cost the earth.

For many people, external lighting does not go much beyond a security light beaming down on the front garden to scare off intruders. Once the sun has disappeared for the day, the garden disappears with it, and by not lighting our gardens, we pass up on a real opportunity to extend the time we can spend outdoors. That is not to say that we should try to emulate the daylight. Indeed, much of the pleasure in lighting the garden is that you can approach your outdoor space in an entirely different way than you would during daylight hours.

Lights (or luminaires, as the whole unit is known in the trade), can emphasize features far more prominently than sunlight. They can really accent the textures, tones and structural assets of hard landscape features much more than those of the soft landscaping. I hope to broaden your horizons by showing you that the cheap ready-made, plug-in systems available are not the only option available to you.

ALTERED IMAGES

One can wash light through a garden to paint an entirely altered image from that which we see during the day. Light can create new pictures that can be enjoyed both whilst actually in the garden itself, and also, just as importantly, whilst we are inside looking out at a space.

Windows become the frame through which to view a whole new world, which is beautiful not just in summer but throughout the seasons. Suddenly, when dusk falls the garden becomes a theatre where everything is new, fresh and full of drama and intrigue. Indeed, light can pick out areas which are not noticed in daylight; hard landscaping features can become sculptural in their own right and distinct moods can be created through different effects. The different textures and tones of brickwork can be highlighted using an effect called 'grazing' which is soft lighting that creates a relaxed atmosphere. It can be used for al fresco eating, hidden in the depths of pools so that they glow mysteriously, or used to uplight or downlight architectural detail in structures.

Lighting depends on you and what type of garden you have, or are creating. The garden size is very important. For example, if you light a very small courtyard, whether you are in the garden or viewing it from inside, the light will be enjoyed at close proximity. The lighting scheme for a larger space needs to be treated very differently. Many people wish to have light to be able to move through a larger garden either for practical reasons (for example to move along a path to get to an outbuilding), or for aesthetic reasons, to view the garden more as a theatre set.

LESS IS MORE

Whatever your own needs, lighting should be considered very carefully. It should be remembered that, in lighting perhaps more than any other aspect of hard landscape design, less is more. In fact, sometimes what is not lit is as important as what is lit. This is because light can spill from one area to another if overdone or misdirected. Also, remember that too much light can be a pollutant, causing a nuisance to both neighbours and wildlife. A subtle approach is infinitely more pleasing on all fronts. 'Lit up like a football pitch' is not a comment you want to hear about your garden from visiting friends and family.

Abstract qualities such as shadow, focus and silhouetting can be all-important in the arrangement of lighting. There are many different types of lighting units to give these various effects, but initially it is a good idea to decide what you want to light and why. Highlighting a view is a good reason, but you must identify where you will want to view it from and what kind of effect you want to create. Do you want to outline your chosen subject? Would you like to uplight it? Would you like to spotlight it as a whole? All approaches will create different moods.

Security lighting Although admittedly important, security lighting can be a real problem to turn off. Manually switched on and off systems can be a logistical nightmare; would you actually remember to turn it on and off?

Lighting that is automatically switched on and off by sensors can be a problem, as badly positioned sensors can be activated by wildlife or cars, and lighting that is on continually from dusk to dawn can be very disturbing to local wildlife and to your local community. You will need to think long and hard about the system that will work best for you and, if in doubt, call in a lighting security expert.

Although security lighting seems to be the most common way we light our exteriors, there are plenty of more interesting ways to create attractive garden lighting schemes.

Uplighting Lighting that points upwards from ground level is very popular. It can create hugely energetic effects. Light can be hurled up the sides of fences, walls, pergolas or even buildings,

and it creates a view of a subject that we are entirely unused to seeing (sunlight, of course, comes from all other directions, other than below).

Aim the light away from the viewing point to avoid glare, or, if you're uplighting from more than one position, use louvres (a metal accessory fitted onto a luminaire to prevent light going in an unwanted direction). The last thing you want from any lighting effect is a beam that is so bright that you are more aware of it than you are of what you are actually trying to illuminate.

above: Uplighting these trees frames the doorway and creates not only a marked entrance but also shadowing on the walls behind. **right:** The lighting here shows how different a garden can look after dark. Different pictures of gardens can be painted by washing light around a space.

Downlighting Downlighting is a very difficult thing to pull off. It should be used wisely, as all too often it kills a lighting scheme, allowing lots of light to bleed where you don't want it (for this reason it is best to have each downlighter on its own switch).

Use downlighting in areas where you need good light to see what you're doing, for example, in eating or cooking areas. However, a downlit pergola or arbour can also look delightful, and indeed, a combination of downlit eating area and pergola can be a useful lighting solution.

Coloured lighting Again, this is an effect that can be tricky to use. If you embrace the whole synthetic nature of coloured light and use it for its own sake, it can look stunning – providing you know what you're doing.

There is no use trying to kid yourself that colour is anything other than artificial. If you flood grass with green light, it will look positively surreal. Whether this is a good or bad thing is a matter of taste.

Fibre-optic lighting Most commonly, this type of lighting consists of a single light source that passes light down a bunch of filaments of either optical glass or plastic to create a mass of twinkling pinpoints of light. They don't give out a great deal of light and so are used purely ornamentally. Because it is only light that is passing down the almost invisible fibres, there is no danger of electric shock, and this makes them ideal for poolside sculpture; they can look particularly stunning when glittering through moving water. That's if you can afford them – they are scarily expensive.

Moonlighting A technique that imitates the light of the moon can be achieved by placing light fixtures high up into a tree's branches and directing them downwards to create a dappled effect by using light and shadow. This effect works best when the light is quite soft.

Grazing Throwing light at an angle onto a wall, surface or other hard landscaping feature will emphasize its texture. Fences or hurdles of woven hazel or willow are a good candidate for grazing because the texture is in itself intensely beautiful and night-time enhancement by lighting will exploit this to the maximum.

Backlighting Sometimes called silhouetting, this effect occurs when the background behind an interesting or semi-transparent structure is highlighted instead of the structure itself, which remains in darkness. This serves to silhouette the structure itself, showing an interesting outline.

Shadowing Shadowing is a technique which really illustrates that light is as much noticeable by its absence as by its presence. It is achieved by shining a light at an object so that its shadow is thrown against a wall, fence or other surface. You can play with the effects by 'modelling' with the light source – moving it closer or further away from the object to change the shape and size of the shadows, and changing the light's intensity.

Non-electric light Of course, to achieve lighting effects, you do not have to stick to electric lighting. Soft, romantic lighting can be achieved by using candles or oil in the form of lamps, lanterns, flares or night-lights. This kind of lighting can be created with the minimum amount of fuss and expense. Cables do not have to be laid (which can be very expensive if your garden is mostly given over to hard landscaping) and the scheme can be as temporary or permanent as you wish.

The beauty of this kind of lighting is in the naked flame and the movement it creates. Flickering candles cast random shadows that cannot be imitated by electric light, and the light can be moved easily to where you want it. You need not choose between electric light and candlelight; they can, of course, be mixed. A well-hidden electric light fitting, cleverly positioned near candles, can give the impression that the candles are doing all the work, and this can create a superb effect.

Lighting sculpture Creative lighting can create interesting and dramatic sculptures from almost anything, if it is treated sensitively. Lighting can also become a sculpture or a piece of art in its own right, and more and more artists are using light as a medium for their work, so it's worth keeping a look out for interesting pieces.

Route lighting There are lights that have been designed specifically to illuminate paths, and they usually take two forms: low-level lights or bollards (bollards are also very good for lighting driveways). Lighting up a path allows you to draw a line of light to a feature you particularly want to highlight without actually lighting the feature itself. You can even create a path at night where one does not exist in the day. Sinking lights into a surface can create some very playful effects.

Lighting water Water features offer the perfect opportunity to show what lighting can really do. Many exciting effects can be created using light on water surfaces, whether moving or still. Underwater lighting in ponds, pools, fountains and swimming pools can look amazing, and lighting up features that are associated with water (such as bridges, decks or boardwalks) will create a real atmosphere. Without wanting to advocate lighting gone mad, if you have water, you can't go wrong in having lights too!

Mirroring is a particularly dramatic effect that utilizes uplighting in combination with still water and it is a feature certainly worth considering. By uplighting structures, planters or buildings around a pool (if you are lucky enough to have one), a fabulous mirrored effect will occur on the water's surface.

above left: Using a technique called shadowing, these lights create a shadowed mass of writhing foliage on the rendered walls behind, particularly when the grasses are caught by a breeze. **left:** It would be wrong to dismiss natural light from the garden at night. Romantic and soft, lanterns can be as temporary or permanent as you like. **above:** Submerged lighting in the depths of water creates an otherworldly effect. Here, it lights a trickle of water and illuminates the water ripples.

MODERN ROOF SPACE

Designed for indoor-outdoor living, this roof garden looks as stunning at night as it does during the day. Modern but warm, the washed, rendered (plastered) walls, stainless steel features and sun-bleached deck take on a new personality when the sun goes down. Using the minimum of planting, this garden creates an environment where the hard landscaping has to work doubly hard.

above: Here the silvered iroko hardwood deck is complemented by steel water features and containers. The dominant plants are grey-leafed to tone in with the silvery effect of the wood. The roof garden appears to be basking in high temperatures and extremes of light. **above right:** A view-shaped cascade of water pours into the hidden depths of the rill below. In fact, the rill is only 30cm/1ft deep but a coating of black waterproof paint creates the illusion of depth. **above left:** Lights submerged underwater uplight the steel water feature at night, as another unseen lamp casts dancing foliage shapes against the walls. **top right:** Lighting creates an intimate atmosphere at night – perfect for summer evenings. **below right:** In the city, inspiration can be taken from municipal features all around you. Here, a spiral steel staircase takes you from one level to another.

The hardwood deck is left untreated so that it will silver up under the baking warmth of the sun, which soaks its rays into the aubergine (eggplant) colour of the rendered walls.

By day the garden feels large, open and comfortable. By night, at the flick of a switch, the emphasis changes. Designed to be seen from inside as well as out, the garden lighting creates an atmosphere that is far more intimate. Downlighting the garden from the top of the trellis contains the space, minimizing the light pollution of the city beyond. Spidery shadows race across the walls as the grasses catch in the evening breeze. The outdoor lighting certainly invites you to step outside. This is a sociable space; the proportions are generous, and the materials inviting. Soft underfoot, a deck is the perfect surface for barefoot, low-maintenance gardening, be it day or night...

This roof garden is stripped down to the bare essentials of a grounded garden. It succeeds through strong design and by employing top-end materials, with an emphasis on high quality construction.

With a minimalist garden, every element of garden building has to be considered and thought about long and hard before committing to a final design. Here, clean lines dominate the space. The horizontal slatted trellis, designed to keep the world out and the garden in, still allows as much light as possible to enter the outdoor room. Glass is used to reflect the windows of the skyline beyond the garden's perimeter, with the clear panes imitated by the deck-level rill that surrounds them.

Although the materials are manufactured, they are stripped down in their application, to appear as simple and natural as possible.

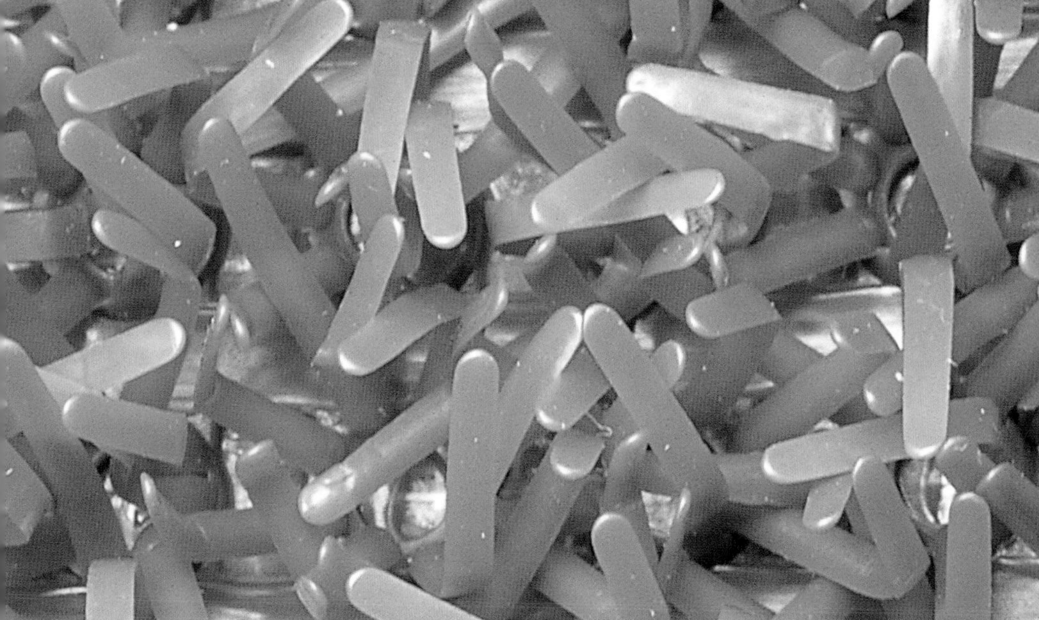

PART 3

MATERIALS SOURCEBOOK

Having considered the hows, wheres and whys of hard landscape materials and how they can best work for you in your garden, you will probably already have a strong feeling about what type of materials you want to use.

Pin-pointing which type of timber or what kind of brick or how you would like a product to be finished is often the hardest choice of all. There are thousands of products on the market to consider before you can decide on the material that will work best for your garden, and to give strength to the style or look you want to achieve.

I hope Part 3 will act as a sourcebook for your ideas and that it will make your mouth water that little bit more before you finally extinguish all options and make your final choice of materials. With swatches of products, together with the details of the suppliers that manufacturer them, I hope Part 3 will let you get your hands on exactly what you've been looking for.

For supplies in the US or Canada, contact a home improvement store in your area (we've supplied home office information for finding the store closest to you on page 192) or check your phone directory for local suppliers and contractors.

STONE

Stone is the oldest building material known to man. It intrinsically links us to the earth and is steeped with such spirituality and history that working with stone, large or small, links you with the past. Stone feels good.

The garden environment offers a wealth of applications for stone in some shape or form. Whether it is a traditional or modern space, raw or finished stone fits easily into any space. Working well with plants and in combination with other hard landscape materials, even the newest piece of rock seamlessly blends into the garden with time. The stone type you use, and the way in which you use it, will be governed by the overall style of your space. Because of the surrounding environment of a garden local stone always works best, as it will naturally blend into an area it is already accustomed to. However, the application or role of stone as a landscaping material is ultimately down to personal choice and taste.

STONE AS SCULPTURE

Statutory and sculptural pieces that have been hewn from solid rock are preferable to the reconstituted stone often found in garden centre versions. Although the quality of reconstituted stone pieces is improving rapidly, genuine stone features are more honest and they don't need to try hard to please.

Architectural salvage and garden reclamation yards, as well as antique shops, often yield the genuine article at reasonable prices. But, if you still can't find what you're looking for, then stone yards or quarries should be the next port of call. There really is something mysteriously enticing about a quarry. Pinched into the hillsides, quarries have mined stones piled up in vast quantities, with fleets of trucks waiting to take it away. If you have the time, then go and visit a quarry and you are sure to find what you're looking for.

above: Quarried stone has a depth and beauty that has taken millions of years to form. **right:** Somehow, stone looks best if used where it's produced.

SLATE RUBBED

The slate on these pages indicates how varying just one type of stone can be. Infinite variations of colour, tone and texture are available in any one single piece. Look carefully at as many types of stone as is possible to ensure you make the right choice.

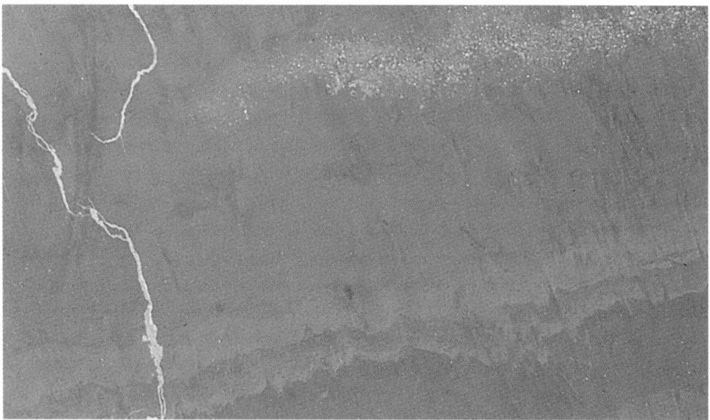

In natural colours as far reaching as purple, grey, silver and red, slate has many faces. Only the earth could produce such a range of colours, echoing the magnificent presence of natural landscapes throughout the world.

Slate, and indeed stone in general, looks at home both in traditional gardens and those that are designed and modelled on more contemporary modern architectural styles. It shifts effortlessly between town or country gardens, ages fantastically, and is eminently durable.

Look out for quarries that are committed to their environmental responsibilities of restoring and remodelling the landscapes that are affected by their quarrying.

Some quarries link up with environmental consultants to ensure that ecological and aesthetic concerns are fully satisfied.

SLATE RIVEN

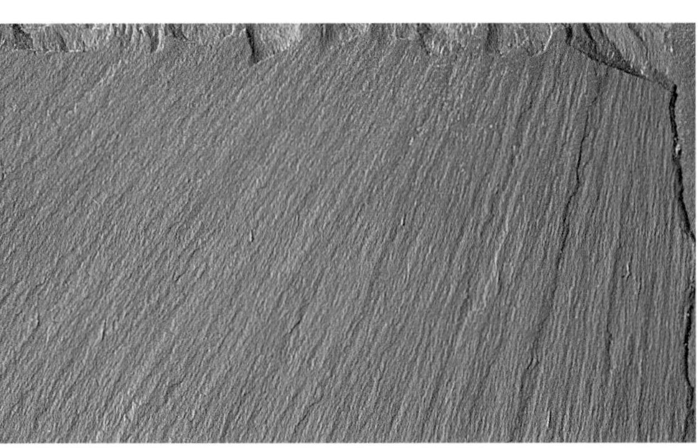

Stone can be given any number of finishes, each providing a different look to the same type of stone. Here, slate has been given a Riven finish, producing a natural texture reminiscent of how it appears fresh from the earth.

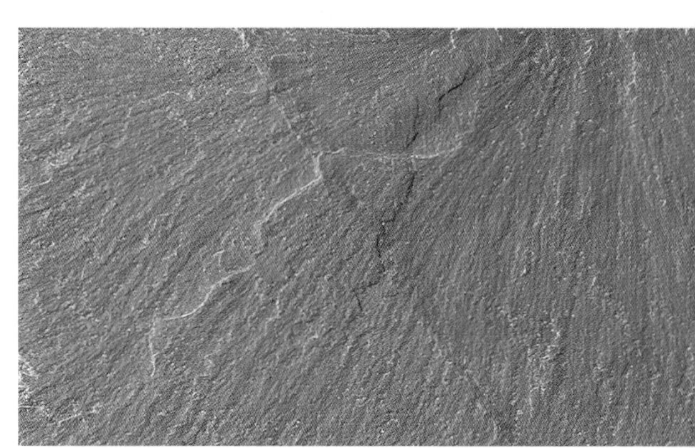

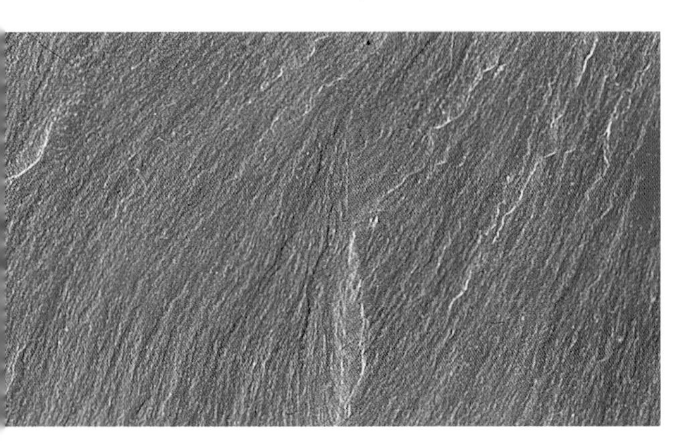

Other finishes, shown on the previous pages, include Flamed, which has less obvious texture than Riven but is still relatively non-slip, and Fine Rubbed, which gives a perfectly smooth, polished glow to the veins and streaks of colour deep within the stone itself.

FLOORING

Flooring probably provides the widest use of natural stone. Visually soft, it seems to melt into the garden with ease. It has a unique quality that looks attractive in any garden.

Sandstone is a sedimentary rock with a mellow, understated tone that gives it a timeless look. At home, in both urban and rural settings, quarried stone can have several surface treatments applied to it, ranging from simple splitting to rubbing and diamond sawing to give it a clean or irregular (riven) surface. Sandstones, of which York stone is one of many, are available in almost any size, but they are mainly supplied as random square or rectangular pieces. The most successful paving patterns work on a random basis, working from a central keystone and avoiding straight joints in any section of a terrace (long, straight lines of jointing will draw the eye). Perfect for large expanses of terracing, use large-scale stones to their best advantage by laying flags simply and boldly. Although extremely popular, particularly in recent years, crazy paving (where irregular pieces of stone are laid in a wildly random fashion) is best avoided. It quickly dominates a space, can boggle the eye, and appear extremely unattractive unless laid very well.

CHOOSING STONE

Your final choice of stone will be affected by several factors, one being cost. Reclaimed stone is usually a marginally cheaper option to new stone and is definitely a more environmentally friendly option. Our stone resources are not easily replenished, so if you can, opt for second-hand stone, but always check for quality as it does vary. Durability is another point to consider. Some stones may become slippery when wet, or can fracture in cold, frosty weather. Always check with your supplier before you buy.

The uneven surfaces of all stone, apart from pricey diamond-cut flags, make laying difficult. The sheer weight of the slabs may be another reason to bring in the professionals, as they are used to working with this type of paving. However, if you are determined to carry out the job yourself, construction details are outlined below.

Constructing a stone slabbed terrace can be undertaken in various ways, but the dry bed method is perhaps the most favourable and gives the best results with the least effort. Working with a wet bed of mortar can result in a very messy, dirty and costly experience. Incorporate a good sub-base foundation of compacted hardcore (broken brick and rubble) or MOT scalpins (road chippings available from DIY stores, etc) and then lay the slabs down on a weak bedding mix of sharp sand and cement. Great care will need to be taken with levels, as the underside of the stone slabs can be highly irregular.

Use your spirit level frequently to ensure a uniform evenness of the surface. Keep a club hammer handy so you can pack up areas using the handle. Finally, you need to brush in a jointing layer of dry sand and cement and then water the whole area so that it can 'cure' or set. You should always lay terraces or patios at a slight camber (gradient) to help any water run away from the house or other buildings.

above: Stone need not be used in traditional ways. Here slabs are bolted into concrete walling to provide a slick garden backdrop.

Limestone is another sedimentary rock that is useful for flooring and walling. However, it is not quite as hardwearing as sandstone, and so durability and frost resistance should always be checked with your supplier. There is a huge array of limestone types and they vary according to region. If limestone is a local stone for you, hard landscaping in this material will blend in perfectly with any other buildings.

Reconstituted stone slabs are becoming more like the real thing and have advantages over natural stone. Light and easy to lay and in uniform sizes, they are also much cheaper.

below: If used in small, modular units, stone can be moulded into any shape. Here it has been manipulated to form great sweeping curves underfoot in The Showakinen Park in Japan.

Granite is a hard, dense, igneous rock, ranging in colour from pink through to grey and then black, often flecked with crystals. Although granite is available in sawn slabs suitable for paving, these are incredibly expensive. Another option is the brick-shaped setts that are often used in landscaping today. However, still don't expect new setts to be cheap, although it may be possible to get cheaper second-hand setts from salvage or reclaim yards. Keep your eyes peeled for opportunities by building up a relationship with a supplier.

In my view, granite setts have a cold, grey look to them, which is not particularly attractive when used in quantity in a garden setting. If you combine this with an uneven surface that is uncomfortable to walk on, you may consider it best to keep them as a trim or edging material to other surface materials, such as gravel. However, because of their small size, they can be used to form intricate patterns and detailing and are so easily incorporated into sweeping, swirling designs. Due to their durability, setts make an excellent, attractive option for driveways.

Slate is a stone I really love. Available in colours ranging from blue and grey through to red, slate is a beautiful paving material. Its finishes vary also, from rubbed, which gives it a smooth, reflective sheen especially when wet, to riven, to give a higher

degree of slip resistance. For boundaries, slate dry stonewalling can look dramatic, as can great slabs of slate used vertically as uprights. Surfacing slate can be more problematic, as it is difficult to fix because the mortars don't set too well. Use a strong adhesive such as Unibond to keep it in position. When laid loose as chipped shale, slate is ideal for scree beds and provides an excellent alternative to garden gravel garden for paths or seating areas.

Marble is another stone to use as a flooring material, but it is prone to fracture and is not particularly suited to a wet, cold climate. When used in warmer climes, though, it is stunning, evoking a grand illusion of Greek temples.

Sand is a material I have seen used for general purpose landscaping. Historically, it was a cheap, readily available material for garden paths. In Le Jardin de l'Atlantique in Paris, it was used to stunning effect over a huge area that was covered by great slabs of rock. In wider landscape use, sand is not terribly practical, as it requires constant topping up to maintain a clean, good supply. However, if you want to feel it tickling your toes, you can build a garden sandpit with a rainproof cover.

Cobbles are rounded or oval, water-washed stones that are graded and then sold for garden use. Bedded into concrete, they can be used over large areas, but are uncomfortable to walk on.

Pebbles are smaller and so can be used in mosaics, packed as tightly together as possible. Laid loose, they have a very informal look, and are very attractive when graded round the edge of a gravelled seating area or path. At the edge of a water feature, they can be used as an imitation beach, serving not only an aesthetic purpose but also a practical one by providing access in and out of the water for amphibious creatures.

When combined with architectural plants, they can imitate the Japanese gardens of the East. In fact, loose pebbles can be used to provide a surfacing area where most plants refuse to grow, such as at the base of trees, or they can be placed over manhole covers and drains to disguise their ugliness.

Gravel and shingle come from gravel pits or riverbeds and they look like miniaturised cobbles. Rounded and smooth from the natural action of water, gravel has a fluidity that is perfect for using in tight, awkward spaces, or in sweeps to imitate the riverbeds from whence it came. Less formal than

Gravel provides a soft looking surfacing material for informal spaces. Use it in awkwardly shaped areas or small, tight fitting spots where other materials would be difficult, necessitating many cuts in slabs or setts.

paving but crisper than grass, these little stones come in shades of gold, buff and brown. They work equally well in town and country, and help to pick up the tones in other materials that are used in surrounding buildings.

Crushed and chipped stone is used in exactly the same way as gravel, but because it is formed from a given parent stone, it is available in a much wider range of colours. Both are available in a variety of sizes and are very easy to lay. Perfect for planting through, care must be taken to contain them at their edges, as both crushed and chipped stone is laid loose and has a tendency to migrate. For this reason t is advisable to lay a more solid surfacing material by doorways that lead into the home, as gravel caught in the deep ridges of shoe soles is easily transported throughout your house.

Self-binding gravels and hoggin are naturally occurring materials that are usually supplied damp from the gravel pit. Laid loose and then compacted, this type of gravel binds as hard as stone. Lay it at a slight camber to allow water to run off.

Walling is, of course, another major use of stone. It can be expensive because of professional building and material costs, so brick may be a better alternative. However, in places where stone is plentiful, walls are more usually constructed from it. Dry stonewalling is a traditional technique that looks perfect in its natural rural environment. However, laying the stone is a highly skilled operation as no mortar is used; the sheer weight of the wall holds it together. With larger stones at the bottom, and smaller ones at the top, gaps are backfilled with small slithers of rock or with planting pockets. Gabion cages are another alternative for walling. These are galvanised cages of steel that are filled with rocks and stones, then stacked together to form a boundary, or more frequently a retaining wall.

Furniture, seating and bridges are all practical applications for stone, but it works best if it is kept as simple as possible. Chunks of rock used as stepping stones over a stream or a great slab over water can look unpretentious and natural, giving the appearance that these great hunks of rock found their final resting-place for themselves.

The parent stone from which gravel or grit is derived determines it's colour, and as any stone can be chipped, the range is vast. Light colours are perfect to lift shady spots in the garden, requiring little more maintenance than an occasional top-up and a bit of a rake.

Easy to lay and highly economical, gravel is an immensely useful material in garden landscaping. Always lay a thin layer of gravel on top of a compacted layer of hardcore, capped with a weed proof membrane, to avoid that spongy 'beach' feeling underfoot. Remember also that larger gauged gravel is heavier than the more usual bags available in garden centres and is therefore less likely to move into unwanted areas.

Sheeting must be laid on a flat, level surface. Simply measure the area required, roll it out and then cut to size. It is available in different thicknesses, colours and patterns but, to ensure that the surface is as hardwearing as possible, go for the thickest gauge sheet that you can afford.

above: A plastic factory where pots are made by spraying the raw material into moulds. **right:** Inflatable plastic chairs are perfect for small spaces.

The problem with plastics in the past has been that, when under bright light, they became dangerously brittle, but now plastics suitable for external use usually incorporate ultra-violet light inhibitors to overcome this problem. However, all plastics will loose a little colour under strong sunlight, but then, so does the colour of your car after a while, and plastic products only fade slightly.

Perfect for children's gardens or playgrounds or, indeed any space where an injection of fun, brightness and humour is required, there has been an influx of products made from plastics and rubber solely for this purpose. Simply look them up in your local phone book or see the Suppliers Index.

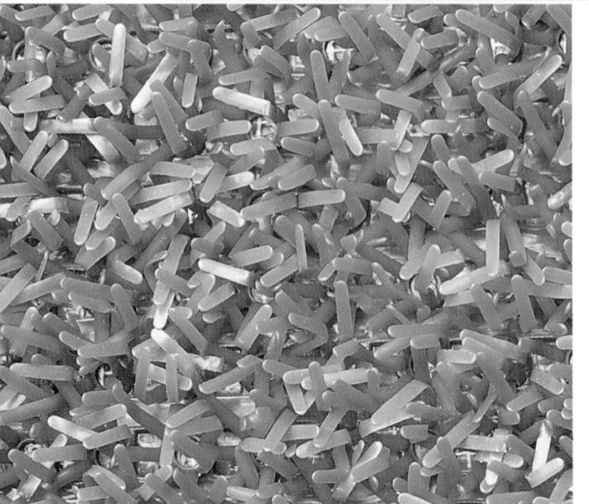

above and **left:** Astroturf® is available in a range of sizes and can be either laid loose or fixed into position. Turf that is backed with studs to aid drainage is ideal. Check that artificial grass is treated to prevent premature ageing from UV rays.

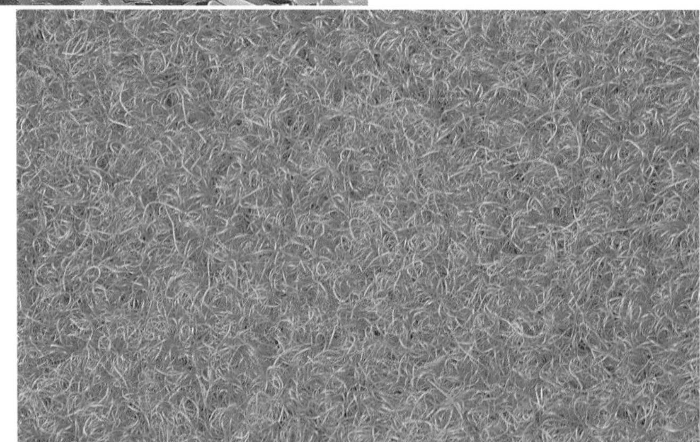

above, left and **right:** The beauty of fake grass is that you can lay it down and lift it up as if it was a rug. Available by the roll, simply roll out the turf and secure for a humorous grass alternative that is eminently durable and never needs cutting!

Rubber matting This type of surface is laid on site. It is first cut to size and then stuck down on to a level, solid surface. As rubber matting usually has a certain amount of 'give' to it, it's great to use where small children abound. However, to get the best effect, it should be laid by professionals.

Wet-pour rubber This is an alternative to rubber matting and has very similar properties. The liquid is poured onto a solid, level surface, such as concrete or tarmac. Once it has found its level all you have to do is wait for it to dry. Again, it is best to leave this operation to the professionals.

Grass substitutes Artificial grass, commonly known by the generic name of Astroturf, is a grass substitute used for surfacing. It is eminently useful as a practical alternative to real grass if your children or pets tend to ruin your lawn. Available in a wide variety of sizes and textures, grass substitutes are available from specialist suppliers.

Furniture Manufactured in moulds, almost any shape imaginable can be created to provide easy to carry, easy to stack and easy to store garden furniture. Plastic furniture is available in almost any colour, is very lightweight and much, much cheaper than wood. In fact, its only drawbacks are that it can tend to look cheap and it can be very difficult to incorporate into a traditional garden setting.

Structures Plastic can be used to coat metals to provide bright, modern pergolas, arbours and furniture. Plastic coatings

above: Attractive and stimulating, rubber surfacing provides startlingly bright results, perfect for children's gardens or playgrounds and much safer than concrete or other painted surfacing.

left: Plastics are available in a huge colour range, and many manufacturers will make their products from colours specified by you.

help provide weather protection and, when carefully used, can enhance the style of a structure. In fact, plastic can even been moulded to build a handsome summerhouse.

Containers Plastic and rubber pots abound and brightly coloured pots provide an explosive backdrop to planting. Available in a wide range of colours, surface coatings can be applied to provide imitation marble and metallic finishes. Imitation terracotta is much lighter and less expensive than the real thing, and can be very difficult to tell from the original. Alternatively, you could use a can of car spray paint to effectively disguise a plastic pot. Cheap plastic grow bags tend to be rather ugly features in a garden, but they can be transformed by painting. Use either specialist paint or a primer followed by a coat of exterior gloss paint.

All the metals below can be moulded to form containers, and metallic pots are becoming more widely used. Unusual containers can be surprisingly effective: old buckets, watering cans or bathtubs, once planted up, can look superb.

Aluminium alloy products are an ideal substitute for expensive cast iron products and are just as durable. They are also much lighter and less expensive. Aluminium-framed chairs are produced with many different surface finishes and coatings.

above: The traditional forge where budget is the only limit to your metal dreams. **left:** Imaginative garden divisions made from plasterer's mesh.

Bronze accounts for many sculptural pieces because of its strong, reliable colour, strength and pliant nature. Lead, although still available, was used more often in the past, but due to its

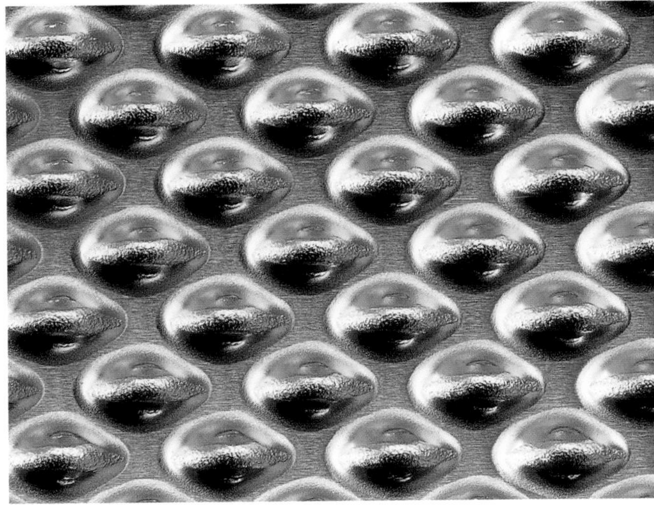

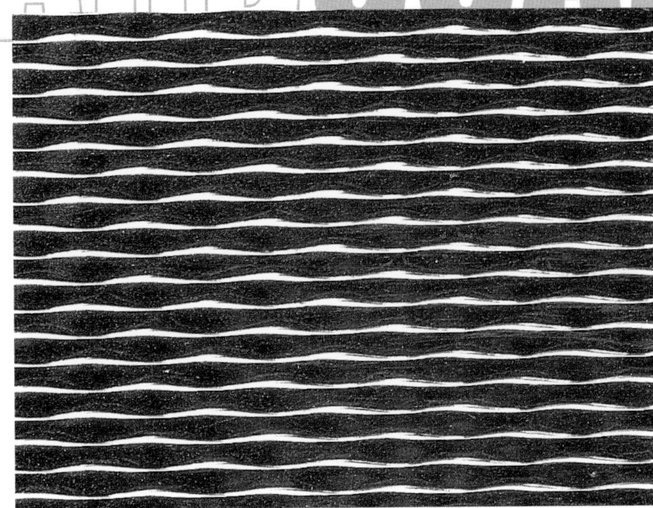

When colour and texture are imaginatively combined, metal can create a stunning effect. The colours of the metal samples shown here are incorporated into the material itself, rather than as a surface coating. Light refraction upon the metal's surface provides the colour, so the hues will never fade.

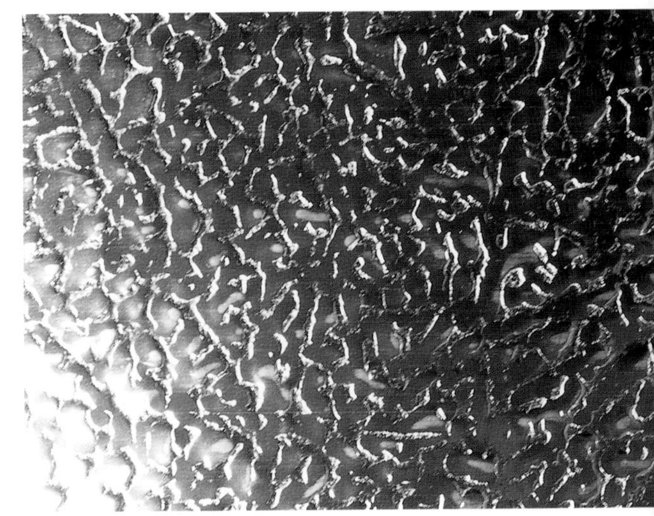

The designs of these metals can be incorporated with any colour or texture; they are completely interchangeable. Manipulate pattern and tone to suit any purpose imaginable.

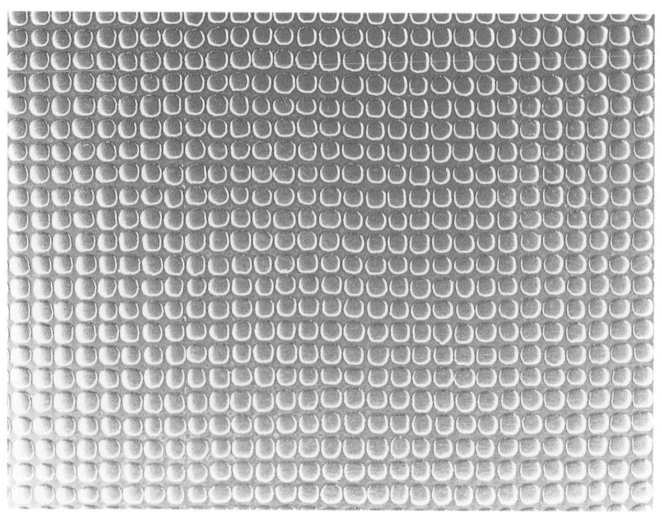

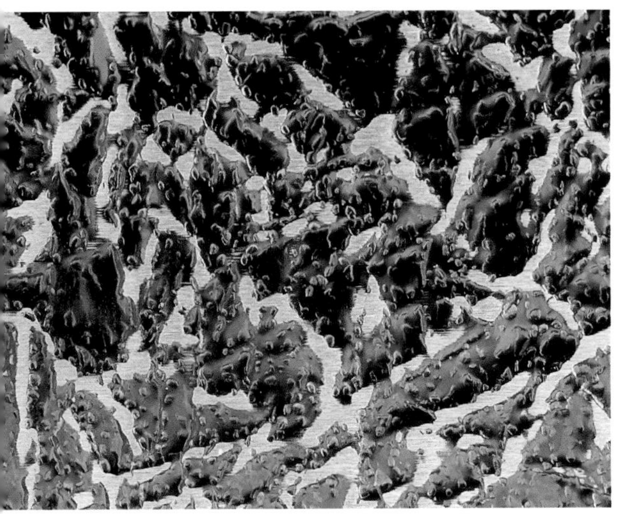

Metal is a ubiquitous material for modern, contemporary hard landscaping. Suitable for floors, walls, garden compartments, furniture, sculpture and so forth, the only limits to its application are your imagination and wallet.

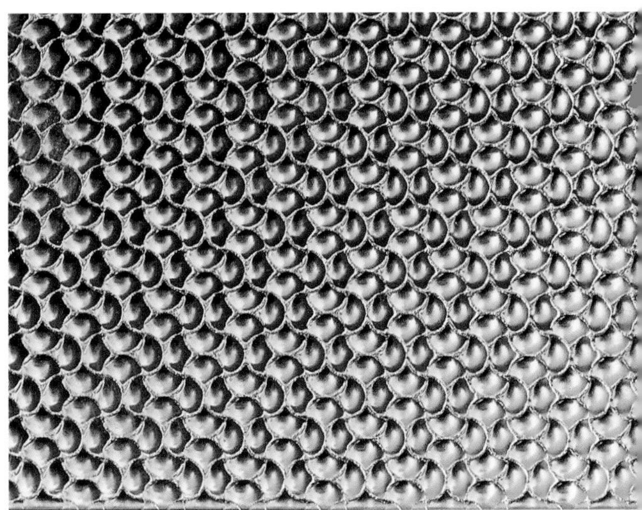

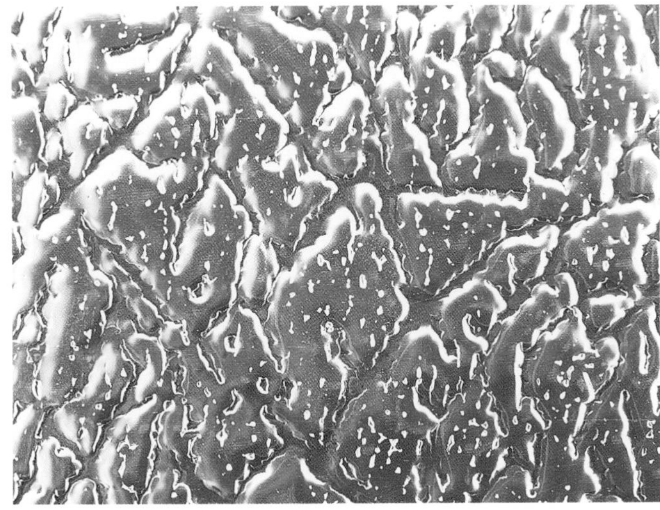

high cost, and the sheer weight involved in handling it, it has gone out of fashion.

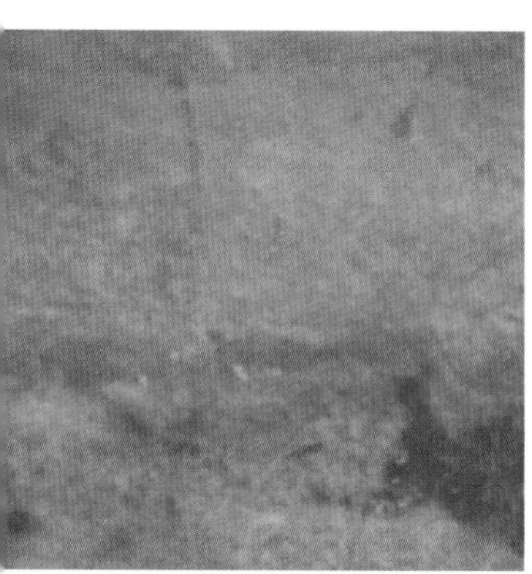

Copper when left untreated is affected by the elements to produce beautiful verdigris surfaces. Copper can be used to make containers, but because plants find copper poisonous, any leaves and roots that are in direct contact with it can result in a very dead plant! It is much better to leave vessels in this material empty, to be used as focal points. But, if you want to plant them up always use an inner plastic pot and ensure that the leaves are not in contact with the outer pot.

Iron if left untreated will rust, becoming red, orange and yellow. Corroded metals used for garden ornamentation are becoming more and more popular.

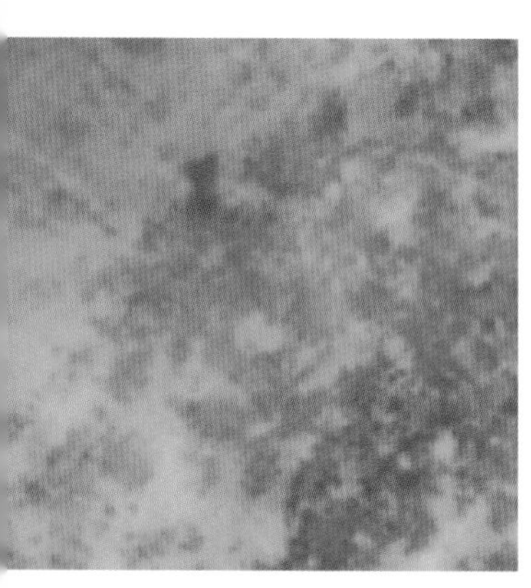

Stainless and galvanised steel can give a modern twist to fencing when used in sheet form or as a mesh. However, great expanses of stainless or galvanised steel can be overpowering – and prohibitively expensive. Using only small sections in internal boundaries will not dazzle so much and will be less demanding on the pocket, too.

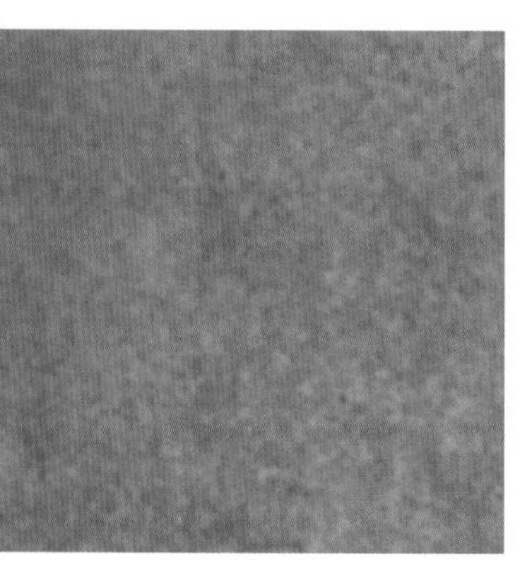

Galvanised steel is becoming increasingly more available in the form of planting containers and can be made into pots of large and generous proportions. Although it is easily manufactured, stainless steel is more expensive and requires more attention than its galvanised alternative. It also needs regular polishing to keep the surface clean. Patterned, textured or embossed, sheet steel can be used externally as flooring, but is best kept to small areas due to its glaring nature over large spaces. Steel mesh is a more satisfactory alternative, retaining an industrial edge but being far less taxing on the eye. Steel mesh works particularly well when stretched over water, as the ripples of the water can be seen through it.

left: Rust provides an attractive finish. **above:** Old cans become slabs and are the ultimate in recycling!

Wrought or cast iron arbours and pergolas are easy to keep clean and can be moulded into the most intricate shapes, They have a timeless beauty, whether sited in an urban setting or a traditional rural garden.

Zinc has a dusty grey surface when it has aged and it works wonderfully when used either inside or outside the garden.

METAL

Rimex Metals (UK) Ltd
Aden Road,
Enfield,
Middlesex,
EN3 7SU.
Tel: 0208 804 0633
Website: www.rimexmetals.com

METAL SCULPTURE

Vivid Space
699 Havelock Terrace (Gladstone Court),
Battersea,
London,
SW8 4AP.
Tel: 0207 498 9001
Website: www.vividspace.co.uk

FORGES

Capricorn Architectural Ironwork Ltd
Tasso Forge,
56 Tasso Road,
Hammersmith,
London,
W6 8LZ.
Tel: 0207 381 4235
Website: www.capricornironworks.co.uk

P Johnson and Co
Ratho Byers Forge,
Freelands Road,
Ratho,
Newbridge,
Mid Lothian,
EH28 8NW.
Tel: 0131 3331824

Fotheringay Forge
The Forge,
Fotheringay,
Oundle,
Peterborough,
PE8 5HZ.
Tel: 01832 226323

METAL SHEET

Metalcraft (Tottenham) Ltd
6-40 Durnford Street,
Seven Sisters Road,
Tottenham,
London,
N15 5NQ.
Tel: 0208 802 1715

RECYCLED CAN FLOORING

Jeremy Dent
4 Denver Hill,
Downham Market,
Norfolk,
PE38 9BE.
Tel: 01366 388899

GLASS

Despite its wide use for conservatories and greenhouses, glass has never been the popular mainstay in garden landscaping. Until now, that is. It is perhaps not the first material we think of when redesigning a garden's landscaping, but it is becoming more and more widespread. The huge range of processes that can be applied to glass in the raw provide a range of applications that produce different looks and varying styles for use in the garden environment.

Constantly changing due to the effects of light and weather on its surface, glass interacts with its surroundings. Looking through glass can warp the visuals within a space, and light shafting through a panel can create a dancing rainbow of colour. Glass can also encase, providing a transparent microclimate within its boundary walls. To me, glass is a romantic, moody material.

EXTERIOR LIGHTING

When natural light has gone for the day, glass structures or surfaces can be brought to life again by the use of exterior lighting. Be it electric light underfoot, glistening through glass blocks or chippings, or natural light in the form of lanterns, either in front or behind a coloured glass screen, it is an effect that should be harnessed and exploited to it's maximum potential.

Different types of glass can be used for different purposes.

Reinforced glass sheets It can be immensely useful to install a transparent boundary at the edge of your property. A bit pricey, I know, but if you can afford it panels of reinforced sheet glass can be positioned to form a staggered effect on a roof garden to stop the wind but not the view. By leaving gaps between the panels you maximise the light, the aesthetics and

above: Glass block structures for outdoor use are manufactured by mounting the glass in concrete casts while still in the workshop. **right:** Solid panels of glass uprights make an interesting boundary to negotiate.

boardwalks over boggy areas, or jetties reaching out into water. They are particularly appealing around water and are perfect for around swimming pools (provided they have a non-slip finish).

Using different types of hard or softwood brings different colours and textures into a deck-planked area. Decks from hardwood seem to melt through sunlight to form a rich, silvery patina over their surfaces. One problem with decking in wetter climates is that they can be slippery, but they can be textured to provide slip-resistant finishes, or rough sawn or rebated.

Materials used in decking don't have to be new. Old floorboards can give personality to a deck and railway sleepers (ties) create a feeling of permanency. If you are going to use recycled wood in this way, look out for splinters and oils that may seep out during hot weather. Apparently, sleepers imported from France don't exude tar.

above: Visit a timber yard to choose your timber. **right:** Recycled timber used for outdoor table and chairs.

Look for alternative materials when building decking in timber yards. I have built appealing decks and boardwalks from reclaimed scaffold boards. Also, decking tiles are now readily available and are laid in much the same way.

If you use new wood your local timber merchant will help you choose the correct type for your decking area and will saw it to the lengths you require, if necessary. Decking is also available in ready to go packs, which you can buy quite easily at garden centres and DIY outlets.

Although a logistical nightmare, due to the expansion and contraction of woods at different rates, I still long to build a deck using different types of timber to create a tapestry of colour and texture in wood.

Wooden setts Wood can be used as a surfacing material in the form of wooden setts, which are small cubes of wood that are stacked, one next to the other, to form a surfacing 'mosaic' of timber – the parquet flooring of the outdoor world. Sawn from durable hardwoods, they give a modern twist to a traditional material use. Wooden setts are available from specialist timber merchants.

Log slices are the circular slices of the tree trunk and can be used for less formal flooring, or as steeping stones through woodland areas. You can either make them yourself if you have a chopped down or wind-blown tree with a chainsaw or they are available from specialist timber merchants

Chipped bark Once chipped, timber becomes useful as an informal ground cover that is just perfect for play areas. In woodland settings, chipped bark doubles up as a mulch for plantings. There is a range of products where the bark is dyed to give shades of green, orange and yellow, but these are exceptionally gaudy, and personally, I think are best avoided. If you want to prolong the life of wood chippings, it is best to lay them over compacted hardcore, but as they are cheap to replenish, this is not really necessary. Chipped bark is widely available from garden centres and by mail order.

Panel fencing Wood is also the most popular choice for garden boundaries and gates because timber fencing is economical and readily available. Panel fencing is perhaps the best budget option, and is comprised of lengths of wooden slats that are either nailed onto the panel's frame, one on top of the other, or woven to give a more attractive option. However, woven or not, panel fencing can provide a drab backdrop to any garden, but with a whole host of alternatives becoming available, more attractive options are at hand if your fencing need replacing. Panel fencing is widely available from large DIY outlets, specialist building suppliers and fencing specialists.

above and **left:** Products such as heather (above), split cane (left, top) and peeled reed (left, below) are becoming increasingly popular. Easy to erect, boundaries made from natural materials blend seamlessly into the wider environment than more conventional panel fences – and can often be a much cheaper alternative.

NATURAL FENCING & SCREENS

Thatch International Ltd
Unit 20,
Stonefield Park,
Chilboton,
Stockbridge,
Hampshire,
SO21 6BL.
Tel: 01264 861319
Website: www.thatch.co.uk

SLEEPERS

Crawley Forest Products
Riverwharf,
Mulberry Way,
Belvedere,
Kent,
DA17 6AN.
Tel: 0208 3113420

HURDLES, HAZEL & WILLOW

English Hurdle
Curload,
Stoke St Gregory,
Taunton,
Somerset,
TA3 6JD.
Tel: 01823 698418
Website: www.hurdle.co.uk

DECKING

The London Decking Company
Unit 6 St Saviours Wharf,
Mill Street,
London,
SE1 2BE.
Tel: 0207 2313735
Website: www.londondecking.co.uk

Archidecks
Trehele Cross,
Modbury,
Ivybridge,
Devon,
PL21 0SA.
Tel: 01548 830022

WOOD SCULPTURE

Vivid Space
699 Havelock Terrace (Gladstone Court),
Battersea,
London,
SW8 4AP.
Tel: 0207 4989001
Website: www.vividspace.co.uk

TRELLIS

Northwood Trellis
46 Chester Road,
Northwood,
Middlesex,
HA6 1BH.
Tel: 01923 820190

TRELLIS, FENCING ETC

Forest Fencing Ltd
Stanford Court,
Stanford Bridge,
Worcestershire,
WR6 6SR.
Tel: 01886 812451
Website: www.forest-fencing.co.uk

TERRACOTTA

Terracotta's beauty has been recognised and exploited by many civilisations throughout the centuries. In Europe, it was the Greeks who first recognised the beauty of terracotta, and the Romans who exploited its potential, using throughout the countries they conquered. Terracotta's literal translation is 'burnt earth', a characteristic that the material keeps whether manufactured by hand or by machine, making it perfect for external garden use. Earthenware as a material seems to sing out for itself. The natural hues of terracotta work wonderfully well amongst the greens of planting, and give the sun-baked look of the Mediterranean.

Manufacturing techniques involve either pressing or ramming the clay through moulds at high pressures. The problems with these techniques are that the moulds have to work efficiently and the pots have to be sufficiently fired, otherwise they may crack or develop other faults. Of course, pots can also be hand-thrown. Indeed, the secret of making large pots is to make them in sections, which are then joined together by hand. To make them frost-proof they are fired at extremely high

above and **right**: Terracotta production still uses the centuries-old traditional techniques in order to produce the finest quality products. In this industry, working by hand yields the best results.

left: Clay is scraped from a pile to make the next urn. **right:** Glazes are available in a myriad of colours to brighten up terraces. **below right:** You can be sure that these terracotta pots are frostproof!

temperatures or glazed with a frost-proof finished.

Although terracotta is available in almost any form imaginable, such as candlesticks, water fountains, mobiles, and so on, the primary use of terracotta in gardens is in the form of pots and flooring.

Coloured terracotta

It is a misconception that these clay-based tiles are only available in a burnt red colour. Like brick, there is a wide variation in natural tile colour, depending on where a clay originates. Although clays suitable for tiles can always be described as earthy in look, colours are available in buff, reds, grey, blacks and browns. There is a view that light-coloured tiles such as buff are as not as durable as the darker blacks and browns, but a tile's strength is derived from the firing process, not from the colour of the clay. The temperature that it is fired at regulates the strength of a tile. Firing temperature also effects the depth of colour, its degree of frost resistance and its durability. To this end, the same clay can be used to give colours ranging from orange to dark red.

Surface finishes

Surface finishes are many, ranging from glazed to stippled, but consideration must be given to how slippery the surface will be when wet. Glazed tiles can be quite dangerous after rain or frost, although if laid as a mosaic (i.e. in smaller pieces), the grout will provide a degree of anti-slip. However, it is much better to use an unglazed tile that has a natural degree of slip-resistance or one with a non-slip surface finish.

Terracotta alternatives

A cheaper, more hardwearing option to clay terracotta tiles is to use an imitation concrete product. Some are of such high quality that it is difficult to tell the two apart. There are also huge ranges of ceramic and reconstituted stone that have been developed to provide a durable frostproof tiling alternative for exterior use. If you have a tiled floor indoors, linking materials from the inside to the outside can give living space one continuous surface.

Pots and urns

Traditionally used in gardens as pots, terracotta urns can be used to give a traditional, ethnic or modern edge to a space. Available in a large range of colours, in a myriad of finishes and glazes, no matter what your garden style is, there is bound to be a terracotta pot suitable for you. As well as the usual places you

would look for pots, such as garden centres and DIY stores, keep your eye out for pots and urns in architectural salvage yards, antique shops and, of course, those you find when you are on vacation. If you really want it, you'll find a way of shipping it back.

Tiling

Tiling has become more and more desirable in recent years, and terracotta tiles can look fantastic in the garden setting, due to the soft, warm, undemanding effect that this surfacing provides. However, tiling can be expensive, and many terracotta tiles are simply not frostproof, so always check that the tile you require is suitable for exterior use. Like bricks, because terracotta tiles are usually available as small modular units, they are perhaps best suited to small gardens or small surface areas to avoid the end result appearing too fussy. Laying a terracotta terrace is a tricky job, perhaps best left to professionals, unless you have a

Sussex Terracotta tiles are made by hand using a technique that has been employed since Roman times. Their tiles are held in sand-coloured beechwood moulds for up to four weeks before they are fired at temperatures over 1000°C. As a result of the firing, the tiles are completely frostproof and can be used outside without any worry as they will not crack under extreme weather conditions.

level concrete surface on which to lay your tiles. They will need either a strong adhesive suitable for exterior use or a strong mortar bed to be set into, and then a strong pointing mortar or grout between them.

Decorative terracotta products

Terracotta does not have to be kept solely for use in flooring or decorative vessels. Tiles can also be used as decorative detailing in walls and water features. The material has become so popular that manufacturers are now producing a wealth of products for garden use. Finials, obelisks, wind chimes and water features are all available from local garden centres.

If you're looking for something a little more unusual then what's generally available, then there are many different ceramists to approach who have more unusual stock, or who will make something to your requirements. Look around at garden shows, craft fairs and in the specialist sections of garden magazines – or even on the Internet – to find a ceramist. With terracotta, the only limits to the possibilities are your wallet and your imagination!

above, left and **below:** Terracotta ornamental garden features add warmth and charm to the garden space, blending in seamlessly as soon as they have been added to the garden.

FLOORING TILES

Sussex Terracotta
Pokehold Wood,
Kent Street,
Sedaslecombe,
Nr Battle,
East Sussex,
TN33 0SD.
Tel: 01424 756777
Website: www.sussexterracotta.co.uk

Ibstock Hathernware Ltd
Rempstone Road,
Normanton-on-Soar,
Loughborough,
Leicestershire
LE12 5EW.
Tel: 01509 842273
Website: www.hathernware.co.uk

The York Handmade Brick Company
Forest Lane,
Alne,
York,
YO6 2LU.
Tel: 01347 838881
Website: www.yorkhandmade.co.uk

HANDTHROWN POTS

Jonathan Garrett
Hare Lane Pottery,
Cranborne,
Dorset,
BH21 5QT.
Tel: 01725 517700
Website: wwww.oxisartists.org.uk

Snapdragon
268 Lee High Road,
Lewisham,
London,
SE13 5PL.
Tel: 0208 8520296

FINIALS

Whichford Pottery
Nr Whychford
Shipston-on-Stour,
Warwickshire
CV6 5PG.
Tel: 01608 684416
Website: www.whichfordpottery.com

TILES AND MOSAIC

Fired Earth Plc
Twyford Mill,
Oxford Road,
Adderbury
OX17 3HP.
Tel: 01295 812088
Website: www.firedearth.com

BRICK

Used as a paving, walling or structural building block, brick works effectively in almost all gardens. If your house is constructed from brick, using the same material in the garden will seamlessly integrate house and garden together. In gardens where the house is constructed from another material, brick seems to fit too, perhaps because they are worked from clay occurring naturally in the landscape. Different localities and countries will produce different bricks depending on the local clay.

Available in a wide range of colours, such as yellow, buff, red, brown, blue, black and grey, and with a variety of surface finishes and textures ranging from rough to smooth, there is bound to be a brick that suits you, your house and your garden environment. Most building suppliers stock a large range and some have brick libraries that will help you select the brick you're looking for. If matching a brick, make sure you take a sample to the stockists with you. Depending on the type of use, or traffic on the paving your are planning, it may be more appropriate to use a specialist paving brick or paver as housebricks are sometimes prone to crumbling under winter frosts. However, this 'blowing' or crumbling can be an advantage, giving a new terrace, patio or path the appearance of having been there forever. Due to it's small size, relative ease of laying, and reasonable cost, bricks are a chameleon in the garden, used in structures and surfaces

left and **right:** Buildings often provide inspiration for garden hard landscaping products. Here, ceramic glazed bricks add glamour and vibrancy to a building staple. As walling within a garden, these bricks would bounce light back into the space.

advantage that they are larger and thinner, making laying easier, and are also less costly than brick. Some are designed to lock into each other to give extra strength, but I find this manufactured look unattractive, although I admit that pavers of this type are very useful in driveway construction.

Another alternative is the strong, waterproof engineering brick but these must be used on edge, requiring larger quantities of these already expensive blocks.

The key is to shop around until you're completely happy with a product. Try before you buy and get samples wherever possible.

WALLS

Brick walls are the evocation of the quintessential English garden, and it is every gardener's idyll to have a romantic, walled garden. But brick walls are not solely used in boundary walls; they can be utilised in the building of retaining walls, internal divisions, screens or as structural walls in garden buildings and other structures. It is best to leave the building of such walls to the professional as the financial and time investment in building all but the smallest wall or structure is considerable. However, it is wise to have an understanding of bonds and basic building techniques in order to make informed decisions when employing contractors.

A combination of bricks used as stretchers and headers make many varying patterns in brick walling. A stretcher is simply a brick laid horizontally so that it's side is on view, and a header is a brick laid end on, so the shortest side of the brick is showing. Walls are referred to in terms of a brick's length. Thus a single-brick wall, that is a wall that is a single brick's width, is 23cm (9in) thick. A half-brick or single-skin wall is roughly half that size, as the brick is laid lengthways, so is 10cm (4in) thick.

Stretcher bond is perhaps the best known bond to the non-professional; it is quick and easy to lay and so is quite common in building use. Only the stretcher or side of the brick is seen. This type of bonding can be a half-brick or a single-brick in thickness, the wider single brick wall in essence being two walls side by side with a joint running along in the middle. A single-brick wall of this type is held together by a capping or 'coping' on top to strengthen it and tie the bricks together.

English bond is a very strong wall due to its very strong joints. A row of stretchers is topped with a row of headers to produce an alternate 'striped' look that runs from top to bottom of the wall. Because a true English bond wall uses this method, it is always at least a single brick or 23cm (9in) thick. Flemish bond is another strong wall where each course is constructed using alternate headers and stretchers.

There are of course lots of other types of bonds, including honeycomb and stack bonding, but these three variations upon them are perhaps the most usual.

CONSTRUCTION

Of course, it is important that a garden wall is strong so that it can stand the test of time, but a stable wall is important for reasons of safety, too. The higher the wall, the more serious the risk. Walls must be perfectly straight and level to ensure that they are structurally sound.

Every wall must be constructed on a strong, solid foundation known as a strip footing. The footing should be about twice the width of the finished wall, and deep enough to support the weight of its eventual height during windy and turbulent weather.

The bond is important not only because of its decorative value but also in terms of support. Bonds are designed to spread the load of the wall through the length of it and to pull all the individual brick units together. Piers, or thick columns of brickwork, should be included in very high walls to add to their strength, as they are better able to resist sideways pressure caused by wind.

As only the outside stretcher and header faces are fired to protect against the weather, a capping or coping should be incorporated at the top. A coping may be made from 'special' or shaped bricks that are manufactured for this purpose, but a simpler, and I think a much more preferable, method is using the same brick for the edge.

And finally, because of the financial investment in building a brick wall, particularly if it is going to be above 1m (3ft) high, I think it is always best to leave such a job to specialist brick layers. Not only will they build a sturdy, safe wall for you, but they will also work quickly – and this is very important if you are having a boundary wall constructed where security is an important factor.

BRICK

Ibstock Brick Ltd
Leybrook Works,
Goose Green,
Thakeham,
Pulborough,
West Sussex,
RH20 2LW.
Tel: 0870 903 4000
Website: www.ibstock.co.uk

Freshfield Lane Brickworks
Danehill,
Haywards Heath,
Sussex,
RH17 7DH.
Tel: 01825 790350
Website: www.flb.uk.com

The York Handmade Brick Company
Forest Lane,
Alne,
York,
YO6 2LU.
Tel: 01347 838881
Website: www.yorkhandmade.co.uk

Dunton
Meadhams Farm Brickworks,
Blackwell Hall Lane,
Leyhill,
Chesham,
Buckinghamshire
HP5 1TN.
Tel: 01494 772111

Baggeridge Brick Plc
Fir Street,
Sedgley,
Dudley,
West Midlands,
DY3 4AA.
Tel: 01902 880555
Website: www.baggeridge.co.uk

RECLAIM

Cheshire Brick and Slate Co
Brook House Farm,
Salters Bridge,
Tarvin Sands,
Tarvin,
Chester,
CH3 8HL.
Tel: 01829 740883
Website: www.cheshirebrickandslate.co.uk

Conservation Building Products Ltd
Forge Works,
Forge Lane,
Cradley Heath,
Warley,
West Midlands,
B64 5AL.
Tel: 01384 569551
Website: www.conservationbuildingproducts.co.uk

Michelmersh Brick and Tile Co Ltd
Hillview Road,
Michelmersh,
Romsey,
Hampshire,
SO51 0NN.
Tel: 01794 368506

CONCRETE

Much maligned in Britain, elsewhere in the world concrete is a well-used, imaginative hard landscaping choice. Invented by the Romans, it was lost when their empire fell, only to be reintroduced as a building material at the turn of the 20th century. And it hasn't looked back since…

Concrete is an infinitely useful product that can be moulded into any shape and used for almost any application. Cheap to make and easy to use, whether formed in situ or in a mould, almost any finish can be applied to it. With a little imagination, concrete can be a very beautiful material; with a lack of it, concrete can be horrifically ugly.

Laid as a surfacing, concrete is mixed on site or delivered by truck, then poured into a mould or footing in the ground. As so many people leave the concrete surfaces at that untreated or uncoloured stage, concrete has acquired the reputation of being dull and unappealing. But concrete can be coloured with dyes or textured by the use of surface finishes to become an attractive terrace, patio or path. Only when the surface has been compacted and levelled by tamping can finishes be applied.

Ready-mixed concrete Ready-mixed concrete is available in bags from DIY stores and garden centres. If you only need a small amount, then add water and mix by hand in a wheelbarrow. For larger areas it may be a wise investment to rent a concrete mixer and mix it yourself at home. Alternatively, you could arrange a delivery of wet concrete from a local ready-mix concrete supplier. Organisation is a must when doing it yourself, as you will be ordering wet concrete in large volumes and all the preparation must be completed well beforehand, otherwise the concrete will start to set before you are ready to use it.

above: Concrete is one of the most often used building products in construction today. **right:** With new, improved products being developed all the time, there's no reason to settle for uninspiring hard landscaping.

MIXING CONCRETE

When mixing concrete yourself you first need to work out the quantities of materials you will need and the purpose of the area you want to cover. Depending on the amount of traffic the area in question will be subjected to, different strengths of concrete will be required and this will directly affect the

quantities you will need. As a rule of thumb, if you're mixing up sand and ballast (stone chippings) for a patio area, path or foundation for mosaic or tiling, you should incorporate 1 part cement to 4 parts of ballast.

Work out the area of surfacing you want to cover by multiplying the length and width together. Most manufacturers will estimate the quantities of cement and ballast you require, based on the information you give them – so make sure that your measurements are correct. Also, it's a good idea to add an extra 5 or 10 per cent to your material quantities to ensure that you have enough.

Once delivered, dig out the area you are going to concrete and add some hardcore to the bottom of the trench to act as a foundation. Now you can start mixing. Use a shovel to add your materials to the drum of a concrete mixer. These run on either petrol (gasoline) or electricity and can be rented from a local tool rental shop. Add water to the mix gradually so the final consistency is not too dry or too wet (it should be pliable, but not sloppy). Remember that concrete mixed in a mixer often looks drier than it really is. Concrete dyes, if you're using them, should be added at this point. Refer to the manufacturer's instructions for the correct quantities to use.

Finally, use the mixture immediately as concrete does not keep and will start to bond and cure instantly. Use a piece of wood to 'saw off' or knock out any air bubbles in the mix that may ultimately make it weak.

CONCRETE SURFACING

Sweeping a steel trowel over the surface of concrete will give it a polished, smooth surface, but a wooden trowel or a wooden float will give a more textured look that will be more slip-proof. Brushing the surface will let some of the aggregate used within the concrete mixing to show through. Different stones used in the mix will give different effects, as will the direction of brushing. Straight lines, zigzags, swirls or other designs can be imprinted, if preferred.

A quality exposed aggregate finish is achieved by waiting until the concrete has almost set and then applying water to the surface with a soft brushing action to expose the stony material used in the concrete mix. You can throw stones, timber, bamboo or other materials on to the surface of wet concrete before it

Reconstituted stone products are now such good reproductions of natural tiles, bricks and stone slabs that often it's difficult to tell the two apart.

has set, but these usually loosen after a time, leaving an untidy surface that later needs disguising.

Impressing concrete with stamps can be effective if used carefully. Imitating other more expensive items such as setts or flags in this way can look gruesome. However, in New Zealand, I saw large leaves that had been imprinted into wet concrete and they looked very appealing.

CHOOSING SLABS

Available in different sizes, colours, finishes and quality, it is worth sifting through the options to get a slab that suits you. An adequate range is available from DIY outlets, but some garden centres specialise in supplying garden slabs and it is possible to see 50 different products under one roof. However, if you don't live near one of these suppliers and you still want a wider choice, you can get samples sent to you directly from the manufacturers for a small charge.

Slabs are available in an array of colours, but it is best to choose those that are in shades of buff or grey. Strongly coloured slabs, inevitably laid in the ubiquitous checkerboard style, not only fade quickly to limp shades, but tend to clash with furniture, plants and everything else. If you're going to use imitation slabs, it's provides a better effect if they fade into your setting rather than start shouting for attention.

If selected wisely and laid properly, concrete slabs will last as long as you want them to. If possible, try to view the slabs when they are wet before you buy them, because they may appear completely different to when they are dry. Also, try and view a broken slab, as the inside gives a good indication of strength: soft slabs often have a large proportion of large stones bound in a weak open mix, and so will crack very easily. Good quality slabs will be dense, with an even mix of fine, crushed stone and cement with well machined edges. Also, a broken slab will show the quality of concrete dyes used. You'll immediately be able to see if the colour in the slab is just a surface dye, which is liable to chip or fade more than a slab that has been coloured all the way through.

Coloured concrete Pigments to colour concrete are available from specialist supplies or builders' merchants. Charts indicate the colours that can be achieved by using grey or a white cement, manufactured for the purpose of dyeing. Suppliers provide full instructions on how to use their products, as their techniques vary.

Precast concrete slabs Laying concrete in its fluid form in this way is the cheapest way to get a solid, strong garden surface, but precast concrete slabs and pavers (see page 167) are another affordable option. There is a huge range on the market today which provide an economical alternative to stone paving. They are often riven-finished to create a more convincing imitation of the real McKoy, but because they are regular in size, they are much easier to lay.

Spanning the colour wheel, pre-cast concrete pavers vary in thickness depending on their use. They are roughly the same dimensions of a brick and are meant for similar purposes, but they do tend to lack the warmth of a clay brick or similar clay paver, although this is changing fast. Again, if you want to buy this small unit surfacing, it is worth shopping around.

Walling with in situ concrete Concrete can also be immensely useful in lending itself to the creation of sinuous curving shapes or walls with large cut-out shapes, by the careful construction of shuttering (a mould built using wood). Make sure that the internal surface of shuttering is lined or has a smooth finish to ensure that finished walls are even. Dyes and surfaces finishes can be used in the same way as flooring, and low walls can double up as informal seats.

Concrete blocks are a cheap alternative to brick walls; larger in size than brick, they can be laid more quickly and at a cheaper cost.

Block paving is becoming increasingly popular as a surface choice because of its durability and vast range of applications, including driveways, patios, paths and pool surrounds. Because of their small size they are more versatile and adaptable than paving slabs.

These can be cut to shape after building to provide sculptural boundaries and internal division walls. It is best to render (plaster) or paint a block wall after construction to make it more attractive, as unfinished block walls can look very dull and utilitarian.

Furniture Concrete can be moulded or cast to create furniture, but traditionally this has resulted in heavy pieces that are difficult to move around. However, modern techniques in manufacturing concrete pieces are making concrete furniture more and more desirable, particularly as pieces sit so well in the urban environment Willy Guhl's 'Loop' chair is a classic example. When it was first designed in 1954 it was moulded from asbestos, but the manufacturing process has since been changed to use glass reinforced concrete. This makes the chair light, eminently durable and provides an attractive stippled finish.

Concrete pots and containers The same principles of design are also being applied to the manufacture of planting containers. Polished concrete surfaces, ribs, textures and patterning provides pots that are elegant,

Blocks can be laid in a variety of patterns, including stretcher, random, herringbone, and basketweave. The blocks are available in different dimensions and in several colour choices to create any style or look desired. You can also use coloured mortar when laying the blocks to create an unusual end result.

desirable and chic. They are perfect for either the rooftop garden in the city or the rural retreat, where more traditional pieces will weather down to give the look of stone.

LAYING SLABS

Laying concrete slabs is a relatively easy job, but the secret, as with all construction jobs, is to keep on checking your work, and then, even if you're sure it's just as you want it, check it again anyway. There are many ways of laying slabs. The most popular are the wet-bed method (where a thick layer of mortar is used to bed the slabs in much the same way as a brick wall is constructed); the five spot method (1 blob of mortar at each corner of the slab and one in the middle); and the dry bed method (slabs are bedded into a layer of sharp sand and cement). I prefer the latter as it allows you more time (you don't have to worry about mortar going off too fast or bother continually mixing it up) and it's easier to rectify mistakes as you go along.

DRY BED METHOD

Once you've finalised the area you want to surface, mark it out using a string or spray marker. Then, of course, you must order your materials and excavate the area.

Before you begin, make sure you know the final depth that you will need to dig down to. This depth measurement will need to accommodate the foundations (variable, depending on the amount of traffic the area will have to deal with), a layer of sharp sand mixed with cement (for the slabs or pavers to be bedded into), and finally, the depth of your surfacing material itself. Keep these calculations to use later. Remember that if your surfacing is going to butt up to a house or other garden building, you must ensure that the final surface level of your path or patio is at least 15cm (6in) below the damp-proof course of the wall to prevent damp setting in.

When you start to lay your slabs, it is always wise to lay them at a slight gradient, sloping away from buildings. This will allow rainwater to drain away without causing any damage to the structures. It's a good idea to lay a string line out using a spirit level to ensure that a fall of around 2.5cm (1in) in every 1.5m (4.5ft) is attained. You can then use this line as a guide when laying foundations and eventually your slabs or pavers.

Lay hardcore to the bottom of your trench, compacting it down with a rammer or a rented vibrating plate compactor, and then cap with a layer of sharp sand mixed with cement. Bed your slabs or pavers into this sand, tapping them down as you go with a rubber mallet. Check and recheck your levels with a spirit level, particularly if you're laying slabs, as, unlike pavers, you'll be setting their final level as you go.

Pavers are jointed and fixed by brushing fine silica sand mixed with cement over the entire surface area, which is then vibrated into a final position using a rented vibrating plate compactor fitted with a rubber mat to protect the pavers. Slabs will need to be pointed separately when the whole area is down, using either a wet or dry mortar. Sprinkle the area with a fine

fine hose of water and then keep off the area until it has completely set.

WET BED METHOD

This method of laying slabs requires a solid base foundation. To achieve this, mortar is applied to a hard surface prior to the slabs being tapped into position with a rubber mallet. This method is perhaps more stable and longer-lasting than the dry bed method. However, it needs a high degree of skill to get the final levels right and it leaves no room for error.

FIVE SPOT METHOD

This method does not require a solid sub-base, although it is possible. For this laying system, spots of mortar are dropped at each corner and in the middle of the slab (hence the name five spot). Then, the slabs are slipped into position onto the surface. Regular checking with a spirit level will ensure that the slabs are level, and you can gently tap uneven areas with a rubber mallet to make them level.

Again, this method requires a fair amount of skill and I would hesitate to recommend it to the amateur.

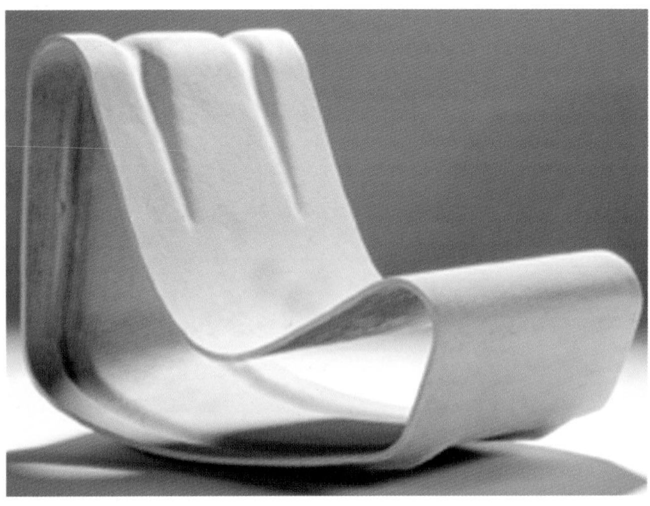

above and **left:** Concrete furniture can be quite a surprise. Designers are creating stylish seating and furniture, whether it is a moulded permanent bench (above) or a light and moveable rocking chair such as this one designed by Willy Guhl (left).

MODULAR BLOCK PAVING

Brett Paving
Salt Lane,
Cliffe,
Rochester,
Kent,
ME3 7SZ.
Tel: 01634 221801

Town and Country Paving
Unit 10,
Shrublands Nurseries,
Roundstone Lane,
Angmering,
West Sussex,
BN16 4AT.
Tel: 01903 776297

MARLEY PAVING

Marley Building Materials Ltd
Station Road,
Coleshill,
Birmingham,
B46 1HP.
Tel: 01675 468400
Website: www.thermalite.co.uk

Atlas Stone Products
Westington Quarry,
Chipping Campden,
Gloucestershire,
GL55 6EG.
Tel: 01386 840226
Website: www.atlasstone.co.uk

Marshalls Mono Ltd
Brier Lodge,
South Owram,
Halifax,
West Yorkshire,
HX3 9SY.
Tel: 01422 306300
Website: www.marshalls.co.uk

Stonemarket Ltd
Oxford Road,
Ryton-on-Dunsmore,
Warwickshire,
CV8 3EJ.
Tel: 02476 305530

WALLING

Lusit Concrete Products
25a High Street,
Stokesley,
Middlesborough,
TS9 5AD.
Tel: 01642 713322

FURNITURE

The Modern Garden Company
Hill Pasture,
Church End,
Boxted,
Dunmow,
Essex,
CM6 2BZ.
Tel: 01279 851900
Website: www.moderngarden.co.uk

LIGHT

Lighting in a garden can transform the way in which you use a space after dark and, of course, lengthen the amount of hours you can spent outside. Lighting a garden at night can open up a whole new world, hiding ugly features and highlighting focal points not readily noticed during the day. However, wherever damp and electricity is concerned, caution should be used, as this can be a very dangerous mix. Always consult a qualified electrician before attempting anything other than the simplest of electrical tasks yourself.

Once you have decided what kind of lighting effects you want to achieve, installation is the next step.

EXTERIOR LIGHTING

On the whole, exterior lighting tends to be of two types, that of 240-volt (mains voltage) and 12-volt lighting systems. If you decide you need the power of a 240-volt system, a qualified electrician should definitely carry out work. Cables need to be buried in armoured cable to a depth of around 45cm (18in) so it is much easier to put in them before the garden is built. It is also unwise to locate them through planting areas that are regularly dug over or cultivated.

You must use a circuit breaker on any power lines and connect cables to a socket inside or to a waterproof exterior socket. It is always advisable to use a circuit breaker if you're using

main voltage (240 volts) outside. If you're planning an extensive lighting system of this type, it's best to ensure that you have enough mains current to power it. Seek the advice of qualified electricians. The scale of lighting should be governed by the size of the area and any plants or objects you want to light. In the largest of gardens, where mature trees abound, 240-volt power may be warranted, but for most spaces, especially small town gardens, a 12-volt system is sufficient.

above: Light can be introduced into a garden to produce temporary effects after dark in the form of candles and lanterns. **right:** More permanent illumination is produced by electric lighting.

CHOOSING VOLTAGES

When it comes to lighting, less is certainly more. Masses of head-height lighting can be bright, obtrusive and glaring. When light landscaping is required, the most stunning effects are those that are understated, gently bathing the walls or subtly showing through plants. The trick to achieving these effects is to use a light and move it around a space, ensuring that the light source is hidden. A 12-volt system is sufficient to achieve this aim, and it is easy to install by the do-it-yourself-er. Indeed, there are kits produced for this purpose, so don't feel afraid of installing this type of system yourself.

A step-down transformer (BS3535 Type 3 isolating transformer) is kept under cover, either inside the house or in a garage or workshop, and reduces mains power currents down to 12 volts. Stepped down 12-volt power in conjunction with a transformer is too weak to produce a shock. Touching a live, low-voltage cable will give little more than a tickle – although I do

right: If you want to light your garden, but don't know how to do it, employ a specialist lighting designer. **below:** Darkness brings new depths to the garden with cleverly placed lighting units.

left: Choose your lighting units carefully. If they are obvious in daylight it may be wise to choose attractive metal units rather than cheaper plastic ones. **below:** Light can make features add drama to the darkness.

not advocate testing this out! Exterior lights are then fitted to a transformer in a circuit. Carry out the connections to the lights from the transformer using the manufacturer's instructions.

Connect up the lights and place them during the daytime, then, when you're happy with their positioning, wait until dark and switch them on. Don't bury the cables until you're happy with the results. With a DIY system, providing your transformer will support them, more lights can be added to the circuit at a later date.

Transformers can be bought off-the-shelf and range from 25 to 600 watts. It may be wise to ensure that your transformer is slightly more powerful than you require, as voltage tends to

drop off at the end of the cable. Also, a higher wattage transformer has the added benefit of overcoming the need to upgrade when you want to enlarge your lighting system.

EXPERT HELP

DIY kits are available from garden centres and lighting suppliers everywhere, with the overriding benefit of saving you money on installation costs. The disadvantage is that low voltage kits have fewer features, such as automatic timers. Also, if you require an extensive lighting system, or have any doubts about installing a system yourself, seek the help of a qualified electrician. You don't want to blow every fuse in your street, or risk a

above: Light is an emotive introduction to any garden space, extending daylight hours and creating new pictures after dark. **left:** If in doubt, use an electrician to install your lights. **above right:** Light creates focal points overlooked during the day. **right:** Water and light can be a dramatic combination.

fire. However, if you want a lighting system that is a little more imaginative, seek out some lighting designers that could design a system for you. If you're completely overhauling and redesigning a garden from scratch, it's a good idea to get them involved in the process as soon as possible. They could have ideas that may be difficult to implement once your garden has been constructed.

As for fixtures, you get what you pay for. Inexpensive systems have low power and provide minimal effect. They are often made from plastic and are not as durable as the alternatives. If you are lighting an area that has heavy amounts of traffic, such as children playing football, or that needs regular mowing, you might want to invest in fixtures constructed with non-corrosive aluminium or die cast metal. Some are very ornate, made from copper or ceramic, and a pleasure to see!

UNDERWATER LIGHTING

Underwater lighting is also achieved using low voltage kits, which ensures safety. Lights are normally submerged below the water's surface. At least 18mm (¾in) of water should be over the lens. Some lights are designed to float, but these can be submerged by holding their cables down with smooth stones. Underwater lights are easy to clean by directing a hose over the fixture's lens.

ELECTRIC/OUTDOOR LIGHTING

Louis Poulson UK Ltd
Surrey Business Park,
Weston Road,
Epsom,
Surrey,
KT17 1JG.
Tel: 01372 848800
Website:

John Cullen Lighting
585 Kings Road,
London,
SW6 2EH.
Tel: 0207 3715400
Website: www.johncullenlighting.co.uk

Reggiani Lighting
9B Chester Road,
Borehamwood,
Hertfordshire,
WD6 1LT.
Tel: 0208 9530855
Website: www.reggiani.net

Nexus Lighting
8 Great Cullings,
Rush Green,
Romford,
Essex,
RM7 0LY.
Tel: 0208 5960500

Lightscape Projects Ltd
67 George Row,
London,
SE16 4UH.
Tel: 0207 2315323
Website: www.lightprojects.co.uk

IGuzzuni UK Ltd
Unit 3,
Mitcham Industrial Estate,
85 Streatham Road,
Mitcham,
Surrey,
CR4 2AP.
Tel: 0208 6464141
Website: www.igizzuni.co.uk

James Davidson (lighting designer)
North Star,
91 St Mary's Road,
Southampton,
SO14 1PA.
Tel: 07000 783873

CANDLES

Candle Maker Supplies
28 Blythe Road,
London,
W14 0HA.
Tel: 0207 6024031
Website: www.candlemakers.co.uk

WATER

Water is desirable in gardens due its soothing reflective qualities, its calming sound or because of the excitement caused by the crescendo of a crashing waterfall. If you incorporate water into the garden, it will quickly become the centre of attention. Aesthetic and practical considerations when deciding upon a water feature and its practicalities are discussed earlier in the book, but with the influx of materials available for building water features on the market today, it is difficult to know how best to choose the right one for you.

There are several ways of building ponds; flexible liners are perfect for natural-looking ponds and by their nature are very adaptable. But in more formal features, or in areas where strength is called for, rigid liners or concrete may be better alternatives. Waterfalls are constructed by interlocking pools over a slope. A pump then powers water movement from a low pond inlet to a reservoir at the top of a slope.

Traditionally, ponds were 'puddled', and although expensive (unless local, good quality clay is available), this technique can still be used today. The pond's shape is dug from the ground and then smeared with a thick layer of clay to give the impression of a naturally occurring pool. This is a professional job that requires skilled labour. Although aesthetically pleasing, the disadvantages of this method (apart from its high cost), are

above and **right:** Whether in the form of a huge crashing expanse of energising white water or a small trickling cascade, the sound and sight of it can be mesmerising and therapeutic.

the clay liner can crack if the water level drops and it will be constantly threatened by tree roots or various burying animals puncturing it.

POND LINERS

Flexible liners More modern techniques employ the use of modern materials, and flexible liners give complete freedom of design. Polythene sheet, although probably the cheapest form of flexible liner, has a very limited life span, usually between 3 to 5 years. Sunlight breaks

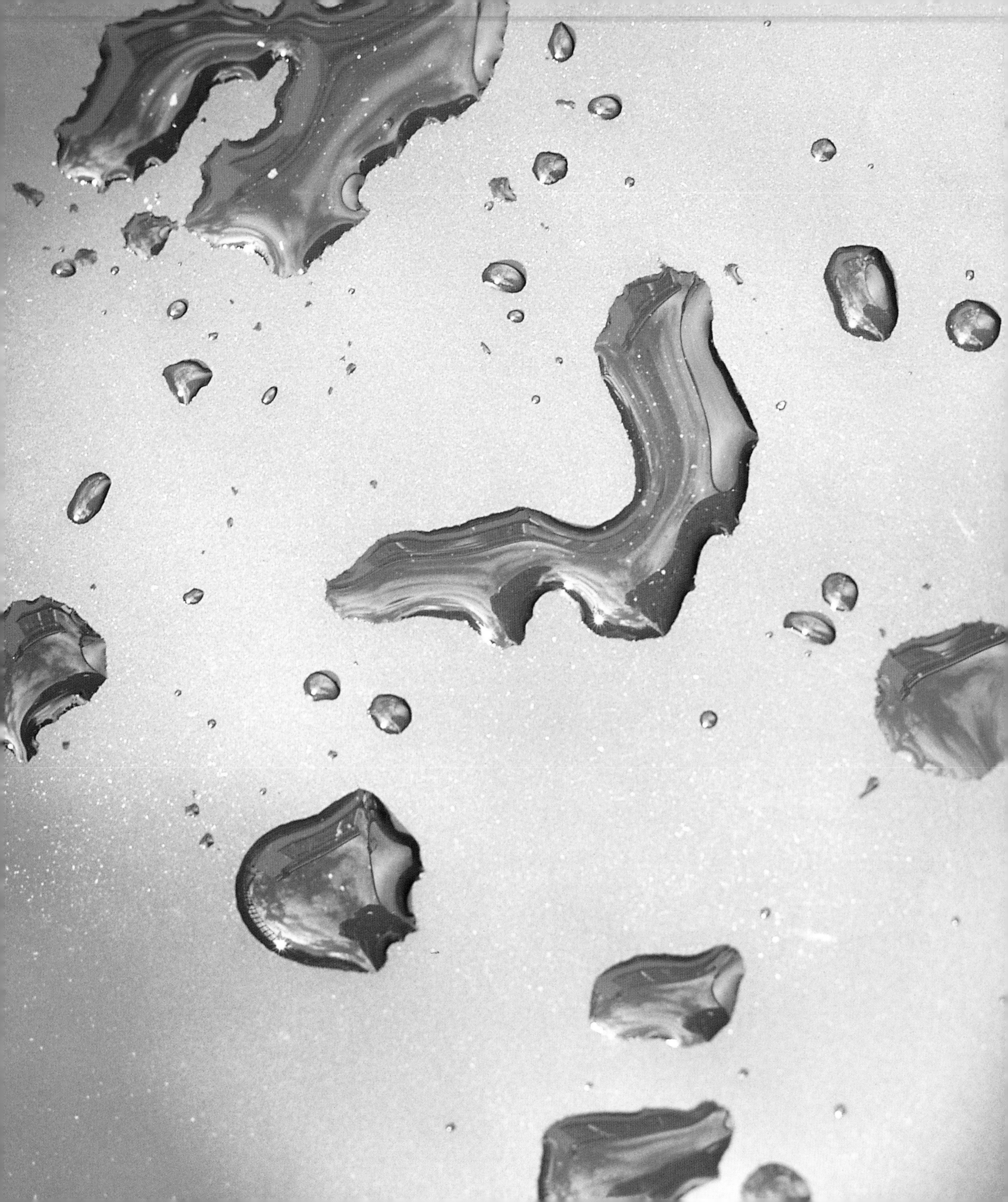

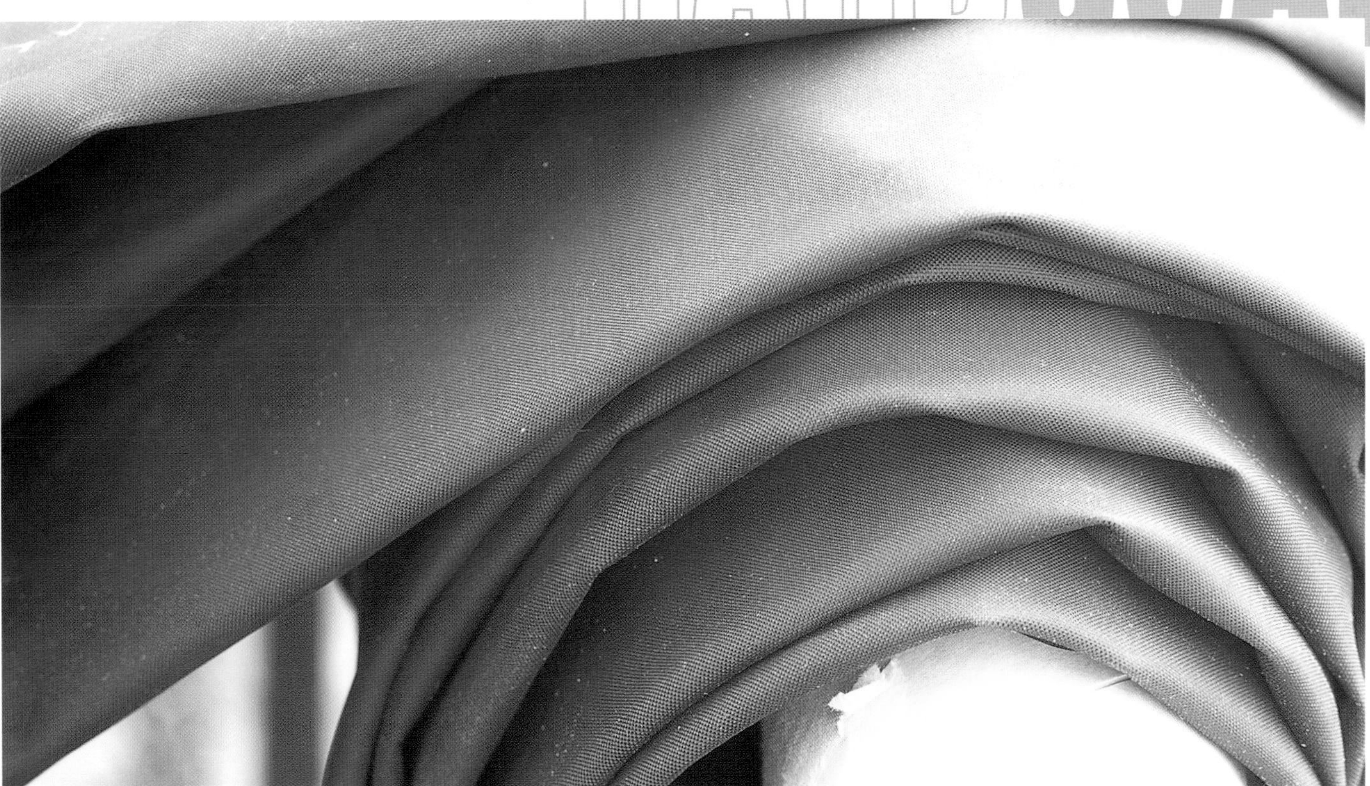

polythene down over a period of time and it becomes brittle and it then cracks due to its exposure to ultra-violet light. If you are looking to construct even a temporary pool, it is still best to ensure that polythene liners include a UV inhibitor and that they are dark in colour. Polythene liners are most suitable for use in constructing bog gardens.

above and **left:** When selecting a liner for your pond, chose the strongest you can afford. **right:** In Christopher Bradley-Hole's Chelsea 2000 garden, water was imaginatively and successfully substituted as a surfacing material.

PVC liners or PVC-based liners vary in weight and thickness. As they can be difficult to mould into a formal shape, they are best used for informal pools. More durable than polythene, the longer lasting nylon- or polyester-reinforced liners may be guaranteed for up to ten years. Usually black in colour, or black with a beige underside, always use the black side face-up. This makes fish lurking in a pond's depths more visually prominent and will hide creases in the pond's lining. Vinyl is heavier and more expensive than PVC, but as it is so rigid it is awkward to handle. It is used primarily in the construction of swimming pools.

Butyl rubber is the most widely used material in pond construction. Measured in gauges, it is much stronger than polythene or PVC, has good resistance to UV rays and a lifespan of up to 50 years. However, it is more expensive. It is a very flexible material, and can stretch up to 200 per cent. Available in a range of colours and in large sizes, it is at the top end of the pond liner market.

POND CONSTRUCTION

Whichever flexible liner you choose to use, a simple formula to estimate its size is used. Disregard planting shelves that may be incorporated into the pool; simply take the maximum length and width of a pool and twice the depth.

For example, if a pool's length is 3m (9ft), the width is 2.5m (7.5ft) and the depth is 50cm (1.5ft), then the liner should measure 4m (12ft) by 3.5m (10ft). If you're using a flexible liner, then pond construction is an easy task.

below: Pre-formed ponds are a cheaper option to flexible pond liners and are ideal for small spaces. They are easy to install: dig out the liner's shape in the earth, line it with sand and drop in.

First, dig out the shape of the pond to the final depth, incorporating planting shelves if required, and keeping the sides at 20 degrees from the vertical to help prevent the sides collapsing. Ensure that the sides are level by using a spirit level laid on top of a long plank of wood. Both the width and the length of the pond should be checked.

Next, remove any sharp or large stones from the base and sides of the pond to prevent the liner from being punctured. To protect, cushion and support the liner further, a 5cm (2in) layer of soft sand should be applied to the base and sides. However, because sand will leach into the soil eventually, it is advisable to use an under-sheet of polyester or fibreglass matting instead, although this will be more costly.

Drape the liner across the excavation and anchor it in place with bricks or stones. Next, fill the pond up with water using a hose, moving the weights as the liner stretches and moulds itself into the pond's shape.

Once full, cut off the excess lining material, leaving at least a 30cm (1ft) overlap around its perimeter for fixing. Nail the overlap into the soil using long nails to stop the liner slipping while you lay a hard edging material all around the pond's edge to disguise the lining.

Rigid pools in the form of fibreglass or glass-reinforced plastic can be bought off the shelf at the local garden centre, and are relatively cheap compared to butyl. Because they are pre-formed they should be easy to install, simply requiring a hole to be dug that matches the shape of the pool. Line the hole with sand and then back-fill any cavities with sifted soil and sand to support it. In theory, this should be simple, but in practice I find this an awkward task and would prefer to use a flexible liner every time! I also find that their pre-formed shape looks unconvincing, often resulting in a kidney-shaped pool that looks far from natural.

left: Water can be informal or gracefully majestic, as this rill in the Showakinen Park, Japan illustrates. **below:** If you want a moving expanse of water, then you'll need to install some pipework.

Concrete is certainly preferable when building a more formal pool that incorporates angles rather than curves, but because it is much trickier to construct a pond in this way, it is a job best left to the professional.

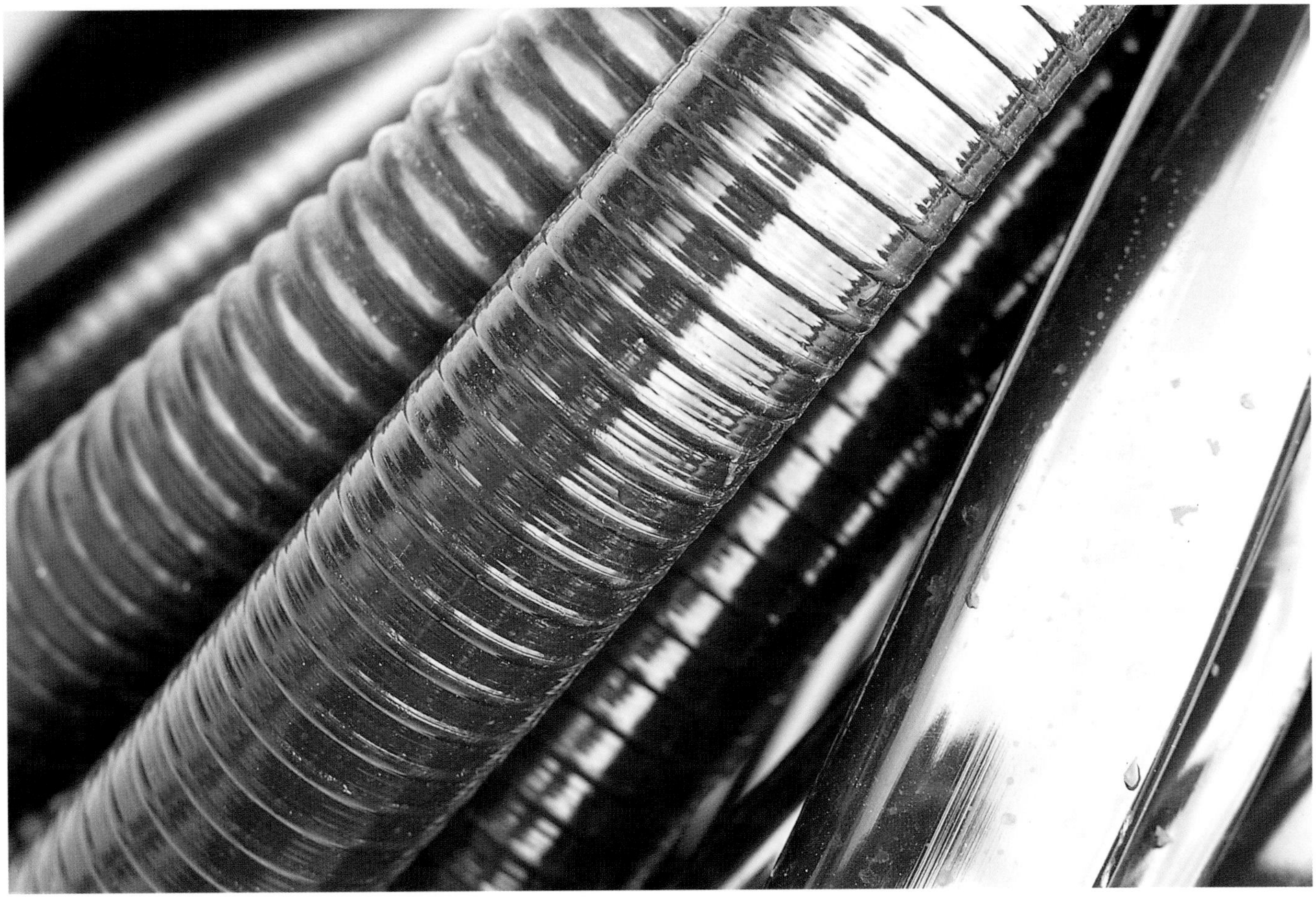

Water in the garden can be gentle or dramatic. Some fountain systems have interchangeable heads so the effect they have can be changed with your mood.

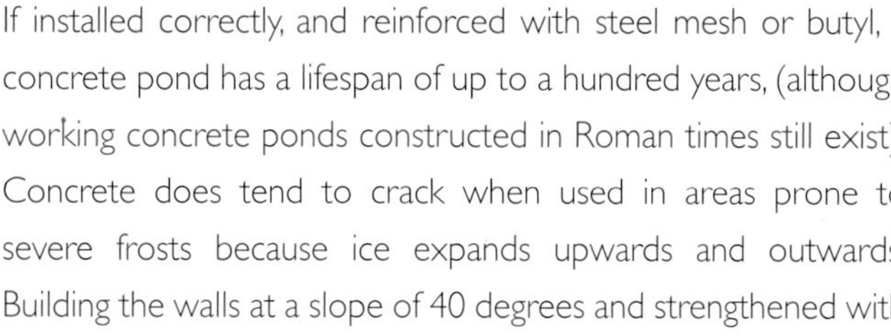

If installed correctly, and reinforced with steel mesh or butyl, a concrete pond has a lifespan of up to a hundred years, (although working concrete ponds constructed in Roman times still exist). Concrete does tend to crack when used in areas prone to severe frosts because ice expands upwards and outwards. Building the walls at a slope of 40 degrees and strengthened with wire mesh will help combat this problem. Additives in the concrete mix or a waterproof sealant are required when building concrete pools to make them watertight, (unless they already pre-lined with a butyl liner).

Raised pools must be strong enough to withstand the outward pressure of water. For this reason they are usually constructed using double walls supported on concrete footings. Bricks can be used on the exterior wall to give an attractive finish, while the interior wall can be built using concrete blocks to minimise the expense.

The raised ponds are then lined with a flexible liner. This is held in place by trapping the edges beneath the coping stones that cap the wall. Again, as this is a specialist job, unless you are skilled at this type of job, it is best to turn this one over to the professionals.

PUMPS

above: If you want moving water, you'll need a pump. Ask your supplier to advise you on the best one for the job. **right:** Larger features may require valves; the larger the feature the more fixings and fittings it will require.

Pumps for fountains or waterfalls are powered either straight from the main electrical supply, or more usually, through a transformer, which reduces the voltage and makes the dangerous mix of water and electricity much safer. If you plan to use a mains operated pump, always consult a qualified electrician and get them to install it.

A low-voltage pump is safe and easily installed; they connect to a transformer indoors or in a sealed spot completely shielded from the weather. Pumps attached to a transformer by cabling can be submerged or surface mounted, and although a surface-mounted pump housed in a ventilated container separate from the pool provides more power, a submersible pump is adequate for most small water features and fountains. If using a submersible pump, place it on bricks to help keep it free from debris. If using a pump to power a waterfall, connect a pipe to the pump to carry water up to the water reservoir at the start of the waterfall's run.

At the end of the summer, disconnect the pump from the power supply and then thoroughly clean it before returning it to the water as quickly as possible. Over the winter, it's a good idea to run your pump for a short time (perhaps an hour) every now and then to keep it functioning properly.

WATERFALL PUMPS

There are lots of waterfall and fountain kits available from garden centres and suppliers, so take some time to choose one that best suits you. Indeed, there are many nurseries that specialise in aquatics and water. If there is one close by, then it is almost certainly worth a visit. Over the winter months (which is the perfect time to undertake any kind of garden construction), many of these nurseries become very quiet, allowing you to take full advantage of employees who are eager to show you around.

Solesbridge Mill Watergardens
Solesbridge Lane,
Chorleywood,
Hertfordshire,
WD3 5SX.
Tel: 01923 284135

Hozelock Ltd
Haddenham,
Aylesbury,
Buckinghamshire,
HP17 8JD.
Tel: 01844 292002
Website: www.hozelock.com

Bradshaws Direct Ltd
Nicholson Link,
Clifton Moor,
Yorkshire,
YO1 1SS.
Tel: 01904 691 169
Website: www.bradshawsdirect.co.uk

Fountains Direct Ltd
The Office,
41 Dartnell Park,
West Byfleet,
Surrey,
KT14 6PR.
Tel: 01932 336338
Website: www.fountains-direct.co.uk

Blagdon Garden Products
Bristol Road,
Bridgewater,
Somerset,
TA6 4AW.
Tel: 01306 743747

Fountainhead
9 Station Approach,
Kew Gardens,
Surrey,
TW9 3QB.
Tel: 0208 3321970

Aquatics Direct
71a Manchester Road,
Congleton,
Cheshire,
CW12 2HT
Tel: 01260 275144
Website: www.aquatics-direct.co.uk

Shirley Aquatics
1355 Stratford Road,
Shirley,
Solihull,
West Midlands
B90 4EF.
Tel: 0121 7441300
Website: www.shirleyaquatics.co.uk

INDEX

Page numbers in italic type refer to picture captions.

A

B

C

D

E

F

US AND CANADIAN SUPPLIERS

The Building Box www.thebuildingbox.com
Canada: (877) 277-3651

Canadian Tire www2.canadiantire.ca
Canada: (800) 387-8803 (English)/(800) 565-3356 (French)

Revy Home & Garden Warehouses and Home Centres
www.revy.com Western Canada: (604) 882-6200
Eastern Canada: (416) 241-8844

Home Depot (US and Canada) www.homedepot.com
In the US: (770) 433-8211 In Canada: (800) 668-226

HomeBase www.homebase.com
In the US: (800) 481-BASE

Lowe's Home Improvement Warehouse www.lowes.com
In the US: (800) 44-LOWES

Menards
In the US: (612) 946-5380

Payless Cashways (includes Furrows, Lumberjack, Hugh M. Woods, and Knox) www.payless.cashways.com
In the US: (816) 347-6000

ACKNOWLEDGEMENTS

I would like to thank Andrea Jones not only for the stunning images she has provided for this book, but also for her continued support and much treasured friendship. I would also like to thank Sue Michniewicz for the enthusiasm that has led to such an inspired book design. Clare Hill for her patient editing and support, and Anna Mumford for her support, enthusiasm and confidence in me being able to write a book in the first place! And, of course, all at David & Charles for taking the plunge. Thanks also to all those people who've let me into their personal garden spaces and to the suppliers who've chatted to me so much and even helped source pictures.

Thank you also to all my friends, without whom this book would not have been possible – you know who you are. But special thanks to Shirief Nosseir for putting up with me through wild mood swings and violent emotion, Michael Kerr for his patience and uncomplaining help, Kathryn Hames for carrying tripods around in water gardens and Trevor Hotz for accepting panicked phone calls! Thanks to Peter Morgan for supporting me throughout my training and Janet Morgan for sowing the seed of gardening in my mind in the first place.

To my family, particularly my Mum and Dad, Auntie Ann, Liz, Angela, and Mama, and also to Andrea's family for standing out in the cold for hours., and to all that have helped me reach this point in my career: David Edgar and John Percival, John Roseman and Jayne Belton in particular.

PICTURE CREDITS

Pages 10–11 Anouska Hempel Design; 12–13 Paul Thompson and Ann-Marie Powell (Channel 4 *Garden Doctors* series); 16 James Alexander-Sinclair; 23 Paul Thompson and Ann-Marie Powell (Channel 4 *Garden Doctors* series); 23 Kaffe Fassett; 24 James Price; 28 Paul Thompson and Ann-Marie Powell (Channel 4 *Garden Doctors* series); 29 Christopher Bradley-Hole; 31 Cauline Brathwaite in garden designed by Ann-Marie Powell; 32–33 (top) Barnes Wetland Trust, (middle) Paul Thompson and Ann–Marie Powell (Channel 4 *Garden Doctors* series), (bottom) Le Jardin de L'Atlantique, Paris; 36–37 plants by Jason Payne, garden by James Fraser; 38 Paul Thompson and Ann-Marie Powell (Channel 4 *Garden Doctors* series); 40 Loxcrete Concrete Ltd; 41 Paul Thompson and Ann-Marie Powell (Channel 4 *Garden Doctors* series); 52 Cleve West; 53 Sixsmiths at Vivid Space; 56–57 Kaffe Fassett; 58 Bonita Bulaitis; 59 Dan Pearson; 60 Brian Duffy at Vivid Space; 61 Barnes Wetland Trust; 61 Sixsmiths at Vivid Space; 62–63 Jardin de L'Atlantique, Paris; 63 Barnes Wetland Trust; 66–67 Bonita Bulaitis; 68 Spidergarden.com, Paul Thompson and Ann-Marie Powell (Channel 4 *Garden Doctors* series), Sixsmiths at Vivid Space, 69 Paul Thompson and Ann-Marie Powell (Channel 4 *Garden Doctors* series) with John Cullen Lighting; 71 Richard Sneesby; 72 Terri Pickup at Vivid Space; 73 Steffi Thoma at Vivid Space; 74–75 Siegfried and Ri Speckhardt; 76 Walter Bailey; 86 Christopher Bradley-Hole; 88–89 Tony Heywood; 91 Tony Heywood; 92 Ann-Marie Powell; 94–95, 96–97 and 98 Paul Thompson and Ann-Marie Powell (Channel 4 *Garden Doctors* series) with John Cullen Lighting; 99 Ann-Marie Powell.